Princesses' Street

Princesses' Street

 Baghdad
Memories

Jabra Ibrahim Jabra

Translated from the Arabic by
Issa J. Boullata

The University of Arkansas Press
Fayetteville
2005

09   08   07   06   05   5   4   3   2   1

⊗ The paper used in this publication meets
the minimum requirements of the American
National Standard for Permanence of Paper
for Printed Library Materials Z39.48-1984.

LIBRARY OF CONGRESS
CATALOGING-IN-PUBLICATION DATA

Jabra, Jabra Ibrahim.
        [Shāriᶜ al-Amīrāt. English]
        Princesses' street : Baghdad memories / Jabra Ibrahim Jabra ;
    translated from the Arabic by Issa J. Boullata.
            p.   cm.
        ISBN 1-55728-801-1 (cloth : alk. paper)—ISBN 1-55728-802-X
    (pbk. : alk. paper)
        1. Jabra, Jabra Ibrahim. 2. Authors, Arab—20th century—
    Biography. 3. Palestinian Arabs—Iraq—Biography. I. Boullata,
    Issa J., 1929 – II. Title.
    PJ7840.A322Z468513   2005
    892.7'8609--dc22

                                    2005021969

Originally published in Arabic as

Shāriᶜ al-Amīrāt
Fuṣūl min Sīra Dhātiyya
by al-Mu'assasa al-ᶜArabiyya
li al-Dirāsāt wa al-Nashr,

                Beirut, 1994.

TRANSLATOR'S PREFACE

Princesses' Street: Baghdad Memories is a continuation of Jabra Ibrahim Jabra's autobiographical work, *The First Well: A Bethlehem Boyhood,* published by the University of Arkansas Press in 1995. *Princesses' Street* was originally written as separate articles published serially in an Arabic weekly magazine when Jabra was in his seventies; these articles, planned in advance according to a specific sequence, described various experiences of his life and were later collected to form a book. *The First Well* relates the story of Jabra's early years in Bethlehem and going to school there to the age of twelve before moving to Jerusalem with his family to continue his education up to the age of seventeen. *Princesses' Street* deals with his later years. Almost one-third of it speaks about his experiences as a young university student in England, and the remaining two-thirds relate the story of his adult life in Baghdad, where he spent the rest of his days, becoming a well-known Arab intellectual, novelist, short-story writer, poet, essayist, literary and art critic, filmmaker, and translator of Shakespeare's plays and sonnets and over thirty other Western literary classics.

A Palestinian born in Bethlehem on August 28, 1920, to a humble family belonging to the Syriac Orthodox Church, Jabra graduated from the Arab College in Jerusalem in 1937 and won a scholarship in 1939 to study English literature in England, where he earned a BA in 1943 and an MA in 1948 at Fitzwilliam House, Cambridge University. On his return to Palestine in 1943, he was appointed by its British mandatory government as a teacher of English literature at one of the best public schools, the Rashidiyya Secondary School in Jerusalem; and he later took an additional part-time position teaching English literature at the De La Salle College, a private high school in Jerusalem, where I was his student during my last two years there. The British mandate ended on May 15, 1948, following the United Nations resolution to divide Palestine into two states, one Jewish and one Arab. The fighting that ensued between the two communities led to the dispossession of the Arabs of much of their lands and properties upon the establishment of Israel and to the creation of about one million Palestinian refugees. Jabra lost his home and job in Jerusalem and was forced into exile, so he went to Iraq to start a new life.

Between 1948 and 1952, he taught English literature at colleges that were to become the nucleus of the University of Baghdad; then he received a two-year fellowship to do research on literary criticism at Harvard University, where he studied with I. A. Richards and Archibald MacLeish, among others. When he returned to Baghdad in 1954, he was appointed head of publications at the Iraq Petroleum Company and in 1977 cultural counselor at the Iraqi Ministry of Culture and Information until he retired in 1984. Meanwhile, his many publications had given him a leading place among the writers of the Arab world. He died in Baghdad on December 12, 1994—his Iraqi wife Lami^ca* having died in 1992. They had two sons, Sadeer and Yasser; both were trained as engineers in Baghdad and are now living abroad with their families, the former in New Zealand and the latter in the United States.

Upon his arrival in Baghdad in 1948, after the Palestine debacle, Jabra discovered a desire for radical change and renewal among the young Iraqi intellectuals, writers, and artists. He plunged into their ranks and made friends with poets, painters, sculptors, and writers, influencing them and being influenced by them. At this juncture, the free-verse movement burst upon the Arab world in Iraq, casting aside age-old literary traditions and creating new poetic forms with fresh ideas for a new Arab future soon adopted and strengthened by poets eager for change and innovation in other Arab countries. In a like manner, a vigorous Iraqi movement in the plastic arts was set in motion and manifested itself in new works that expressed the Arab world's

---

*Lami^ca, pronounced La-mee-^ca in three syllables with the accent on the second, is an Arabic proper name, a feminine adjective that means shining, gleaming, flashing, radiant, lustrous, brilliant, bright and has an overtone meaning intelligent, clever. It should not be confused with Lamia, pronounced Lam-ya in two syllables with the accent on the first, another Arabic proper name and feminine adjective that means red-lipped or, more exactly, one whose lips are dark red or deep purplish red.

yearning for a new Arab vision. Palestine's *nakba* (catastrophe) of 1948 was a traumatic event that affected all Arabs everywhere and shook them to the core. It made them want to change the Arab political systems whose regimes had permitted the loss of a dear part of the homeland to Israel. In fact, a number of coups d'état and revolutions did take place shortly after the *nakba* and effected some change in several Arab countries. On their part, Arab intellectuals, writers, and artists craved for a deeper change, one that would influence Arab culture itself to acknowledge modern times and discard outworn traditions, something that was necessary before any real change could be expected in Arab society and polity.

In *Princesses' Street* there is a reflection of all this ferment. Names of artists and writers abound in it as they related to Jabra's life and activities. This time period can be arguably considered the most creative in the history of modern Iraqi literature and the arts, hence the importance—in part—of this book and its details. And yet, in Jabra's private life, this time period was also one of a search for love. An intelligent and handsome young bachelor in his late twenties and early thirties, Jabra was admired by his college students and colleagues, especially the women, and he permitted himself to be admired. And in *Princesses' Street* there is a reflection of all this too.

The year 1951 was his *annus mirabilis,* his wonderful year, in which he met his future wife, Lamiᶜa , a young Muslim woman, whose beauty he liked to call Babylonian. She belonged to a distinguished Iraqi family. Her father Muhammad Barqi al-Askari was a member of the Iraqi parliament and formerly a brigadier general of the Iraqi army. Her older brother Amer was governor of one of the northern counties in the district of Mosul. She had earned an MA from the University of Wisconsin at Madison and was a professor at the Teachers' Training College, one of the colleges that Jabra was teaching at, and that was where he met her. Her vivacity and cheerfulness, coupled with her beauty and intelligence, won Jabra's heart at first sight, and he made sure to be with her whenever he could and to create circumstances where they could be together. *Princesses' Street* tells the story of this love in the greater part of the book, punctuated as all love stories are with difficulties to be surmounted, pleasures to be had, and the union to be eventually achieved. Jabra's account of courting her is delightful and makes for pleasant reading.

In *The First Well* he spoke of childhood in a style that was most simple in order to create the atmosphere of a child's innocence, his wonder at the world around him, and his yearning for discovery and learning. In *Princesses' Street* Jabra's style was much different, for he was now a man in his seventies looking back at his exuberant thirties with the imagination of a writer who had written about love in fiction and poetry after having read and translated some of the world's masterpieces on love.

Princesses' Street is the last book that Jabra published during his lifetime. It appeared in the fall of 1994, and he died, as mentioned above, on December 12, 1994. In the previous two years, he was finalizing poems for the publication of his fourth collection, but he did not live to see it published. In a letter dated December 21, 1993, he wrote to me from Baghdad saying, "25 poems I composed in the second half of last year are perhaps the most beautiful poems that I have ever written in my life. I have intentionally delayed publishing them in a book but most probably they will be published in the middle of next year." They were actually published posthumously in 1996 under the title of *A Sequence of Poems: Some for Her Phantasm, and Some for Her Body,* with a preface by the Iraqi poet, Dr. Abd al-Wahid Lulua. They are indeed his most beautiful poems and some of the best Arabic love poetry written in recent years. Although the beloved is nowhere mentioned by name in them, she is none other than Lamiᶜa, his great love.

Princesses' Street helps us understand not only Jabra and his great love but also his times in Iraq when the country was enjoying a moderate kind of democracy under the growth of middle class and bourgeois values prevalent before the advent of the one-party system, which Saddam Hussein later highjacked. In *Princesses' Street,* names of Iraqi personalities who crossed Jabra's life are abundant—leaders in politics, economics, administration, education; men and women who played important roles in Iraq's development; colleagues, friends, and former students of his who rose to high positions in Iraq and influenced its growing modernizing society. And all of them are part of the history of modern Iraq. If Iraq is today suffering from turmoil and a variety of painful experiences after the removal of the tyrannical rule of Saddam Hussein, it can rightfully look forward to instituting a real democracy in the near future and a return to the halcyon days when it was a source of Arab pride because of its people's creativity in literature and the arts, let alone many other fields.

Montreal, February 5, 2005

TRANSLATOR'S NOTE
ON DIACRITICAL MARKS

As in *The First Well,* I abandoned all diacritics in transliterating Arabic words and proper names in *Princesses' Street* in an effort to make them easier to read. In the former book, this was at Jabra's request; in the latter, at the publisher's—after Jabra's death—out of respect for his express intention when he was alive.

Princesses' Street

AUTHOR'S PREFACE

When I thought of writing this book, I was responding to a request of a friend of mine who was the chief editor of a widely circulated weekly magazine. He suggested that I write a number of articles for him, each describing one of my life experiences. I therefore summoned up from memory events to narrate in detail as stories from my life—and what life is devoid of interesting and important stories if their narrator knows how to tell them? I did not begin telling the first story until I had made a list, brief though it was, of a number of personal events that I considered to be significant and that could be connected one to another to constitute, in the end, a kind of autobiography.

My autobiographical book, *The First Well,** had been published earlier, and I was surprised by the great interest in it as readers began asking me to continue it—for I had stopped the story in it on my reaching the age of thirteen, knowing that events of adolescence and the beginning of maturity must necessarily be narrated and treated differently.

I found out that, if I placed my "stories" in a conventional time sequence, they would achieve part of my aim. However, in that particular period of my life I was preoccupied with events, life situations, and intellectual concerns that required my exploring and crystallizing them on paper. Furthermore, I was busy making enjoyable trips and attending inter-Arab and international conferences that made me feel that by participating in them I was continuing in the attempt to write my autobiography. My novel, *Diaries of Sarab Affan,* and the articles in my books, *Meditations on a Marble Structure* and *Living with the Tigress, and Other Papers,* as well as my dialogues with interviewers published in *Exploration and Wonder*—all of which appeared after *The First Well*—were nothing but a kind of an indirect continuation of my autobiography.

---

*Translated into English by Issa J. Boullata as *The First Well: A Bethlehem Boyhood* (Fayetteville: University of Arkansas Press, 1995), it won the inaugural University of Arkansas Press Award for Arabic Literature in Translation, offered for the first time in 1993. *(Translator's note.)*

3

However, I was aware that there was a period of my life that had not received its rightful share of my attention, and I had to attend to it—despite the difficulty of going through all its details—for it contained the greatest turning point of my life, both private and public. This period was the early 1950s when I first came to Baghdad.

All of a sudden, I realized that 1951, the year Lami͑a and I had met in early spring, was a period in which the events and the formation of close personal relationships, even after this long time, appeared to me amazing and intense in their wonder and significance, and their effect continued throughout the 1950s. This period is one which many people in Baghdad today remember as a golden age with its creative aspirations and eagerness for change and modernization, and they try to recall its magic before it disappears, appearing as one of the richest in contemporary Arab society.

And thus in chapter 6, I speak about only some of what is possible to speak about in this regard. Life continues daily to develop and have new stories and wonders that seize our souls, our minds, and our hearts. Meanwhile, with all the new stories and wonders, we don't know where exactly to start or where to end—or rather we know that they start and that they do not end.

al-Mansour, Baghdad
March 18, 1994
Jabra Ibrahim Jabra

1

The First Trip

I was nineteen years old when I arrived at Port Said after a long night's ride by train from the city of Jaffa. That was the first time I had traveled from of my hometown to the larger horizons of the world, and I was full of enthusiasm for everything that would excite my eyes and my mind.

England and France had declared war on Germany on September 3, 1939, and thus the Second World War started only twenty-one years after the end of the First World War. On that day, Ali Kamal (who later became a psychiatrist) and I were in Jerusalem trying to gather information from radio newscasts. I imagined that in a week or two war would spread all over Europe, and I was sure that my opportunity to travel to England on scholarship would be lost immediately. I had prepared myself for about one year, teaching at a miserable elementary school and spending the rest of my time in reading, writing, and translating and in painfully treating my eyes in order to get rid of the ophthalmia that had prevented me from traveling the year before. And I had healed.

However, the officials at the Department of Education in Jerusalem put my thoughts at ease when they told me that, despite the beginning of war, the scholarship was still on if I was ready to travel. Images of bombs falling like a devastating rain on English and European cities came to mind, and my parents insisted that I should refuse to go until the war ended. But I was not afraid and insisted that I should proceed with my plans, saying, "In facing the probable woes of this war, I will be like millions of other people. I am no better than they are!"

My mother especially was not convinced of this logic, and

she continued to object, and weep. But when she found out that my father, my brothers, and my grandmother had stopped resisting me, she grudgingly agreed to my determined wish and stopped crying.

The Department of Education made travel arrangements to England for me and two other students through the office of Thomas Cook. The other students were Hilmi Samara, who was about two years younger than I was, and Hamid Attari, who was three years my elder. We were all graduates of the Arab College in Jerusalem, that fine institution in which the education authorities gathered the outstanding young men from all the government schools in Palestine; beginning at age fifteen, these young men studied for two or three years in the hands of capable teachers under the supervision of a dean who was one of the most prominent thinkers of Palestine, namely, Professor Ahmad Samih al-Khalidi. When they graduated, they became schoolteachers or were sent on scholarship to the American University of Beirut or to universities in England, for in those days there wasn't a single university in the whole of Palestine.

The itinerary was that we would go by car from Jerusalem to Lydda and take the train from there to Jaffa and in a night trip proceed to Rafah then Qantara and hence to Port Said, which we would reach at dawn. After two or three days in Port Said, we would board the Japanese ship *Suwa Maro,* which would take us to Naples and Marseilles, through the Strait of Gibraltar northward into the Atlantic Ocean. We would then sail across the Bay of Biscay, noted for its turbulent waters, to the English Channel and dock at Dover. From there we would go to London; then each one of us would go his own way to the city where his university was.

We had chosen a Japanese ship on purpose. Japan was still neutral in the war, and so was Italy for that matter, and Japanese ships could enter any port they liked. However, we knew that we would still be exposed to certain dangers during more than twenty-five days of travel and encounters with the unknown.

It was not long before we were surprised at the sight of the French engineer who toward the end of the last century had entered Arab history through the wide door of Egyptian history, namely, Ferdinand de Lesseps.

On our first day in Port Said, we went to stay at an old hotel. We were worried about the safety of our luggage, meager as it was, because our relatives and friends had relentlessly advised us to protect our belongings from the pickpockets and swindlers who they claimed teemed in the ports of the Mediterranean Sea and who would definitely try to take advantage of our innocence and ignorance. However, on arrival we were only met by the many shouting men of playful and jocular dispositions announcing their hotels, who snatched the train passengers and put them in waiting taxicabs that took them where they wanted. We were not opposed to that as long as, in the end, we found a place to stay, rooms of some sort—damp and miserable—that we could tolerate for two or three nights until the *Suwa Maro* arrived.

In point of fact, I was not very much worried about my suitcase, for it was small and stuffed with books and papers, feeling that only people like me and my two companions would care for such things. (When I returned from England a few years later, having shipped my belongings separately in several suitcases, I found that all my clothes had been taken from them; yet my books, several hundreds of them, had not been touched except for one by Rabelais, which I don't know why the thief had been tempted to steal.)

The three of us hastened to leave the hotel to wander about in the streets of Port Said and sit at its cafés. When we were having lunch at one of the restaurants, we talked about the history of the city as much as our memories of it permitted. A few days earlier in Jerusalem and in preparation for the short period we would spend in Port Said, I had gone over the many details of the opening of the Suez Canal, which had caused the establishment of this port during the rule of Said Pasha, the ruler of Egypt, who had given his name to the city. We discovered that, on the day of our arrival, we could almost celebrate the seventieth anniversary of the Suez Canal; for it had been opened at the beginning of October 1869 by the man succeeding Said in ruling Egypt, Khedive Ismail Pasha, and the opening was the occasion for celebrations rarely matched in history for their luxury, their magnificence, and their extravagance.

In those days, Ismail was in the prime of his manhood, almost forty years of age, and wanted to gather the kings and princes of Europe at the opening festival in order to announce to the world that henceforth Egypt was no longer part of Africa and that it had become part of Europe. To emphasize his independence from Istanbul, he did not invite representatives of Sultan Abd al-Aziz to the opening despite the umbilical cord that was still officially present between the khedive in Egypt and the Sublime Porte in Istanbul, capital of the Ottoman Empire.

Being attracted by the sea, we headed for the port after lunch, and some people directed us to the place where we could hire a boat that would take us to the entrance of the canal where we could see a large statue of Ferdinand de Lesseps, who with his intelligence and illustrious reputation had convinced Said Pasha of the importance of digging the canal that would unite two seas. He told him of the vision in which he saw a great rainbow linking the shining East and the gloomy West burdened with clouds. Said charged him with realizing his vision, so he designed the canal, drew its plans, and implemented them with genius. That took him fifteen years of continuous work, which started in Said's rule and ended in that of his nephew Ismail, son of Ibrahim Pasha, who was the first to assume the title of khedive two years before the opening of the canal.

We found a small boat with one sail that reminded us of Muhammad Abd al-Wahhab's song "The Boat and the Sailor." The boatman said he would charge us ten piasters to take us to the canal and its statue, and we agreed. We boarded his boat, happy at a cruise that would combine the beauties of the sea and of history, while the sun shone and its rays danced and glimmered on the gentle waves.

As the boatman rowed with ease and strength and the boat swayed soothingly and freely, we went over further details of the history of the canal in our conversation. Khedive Ismail's aim was to make the European states, especially France, admire what he had achieved in his desire of getting their support for his political ambitions. He hoped that Emperor Napoleon III and his wife Eugénie would attend the opening ceremonies, but the emperor was sick and apologized, but the empress came alone in her most magnificent finery, still possessing a great deal of beauty although she was over forty. De Lesseps had a role in persuading her to come because he was related to her, and they both had roots in Spain. She was interested in coming to Egypt to meet another great guest, namely, the emperor of the Austro-Hungarian empire; for she hoped she could persuade him to distance himself from Germany and ally himself with France, which was then facing the German threat posed by Bismarck—a threat that caused the empress, a few months after she returned to Paris, to make her husband declare war on Germany. The war brought disaster upon France and ended the reign of Napoleon III and his beautiful empress, and France could no longer call itself an empire as it lost control of Alsace and Lorraine for approximately half a century.

We brought to mind many of the strange things related to the amazing, historic opening of the canal, including the forty-two palaces which the khedive built for his visiting luminaries. We particularly mused about the large palace he specifically constructed as a residence for Eugénie on the bank of the Nile in Cairo (which was renovated in recent years to become a Marriott Hotel). We also mentioned the opera house that he wanted to open with the opera Aïda, specially composed for the occasion by Giuseppe Verdi, the greatest Italian musician of the time. Aïda is set in ancient Egypt, but it was not completed in time, and instead Verdi offered Rigoletto, which was based on a play by Victor Hugo. As a consequence of all those wonderful ceremonies, Egypt was burdened with heavy debts, causing Ismail to abdicate ten years later and Britain to occupy Egypt in an almost incredible series of events!

However, as our boat rocked on the waves bringing us nearer to the monument of de Lesseps, our conversation concentrated on the great engineer's odious behavior. With or without the khedive's approval, he drove the tens of thousands of Egyptians digging the canal like slaves. They had to work in a sort of corvée, for no wages except for some food to sustain their energy in order that they could continue digging. The region was a terrible, pestilence-ridden one in which the desert interpenetrated swampy lands and marshes, and thousands of workers died of disease and exhaustion over the years. We then posed the question that young people always ask when they begin to face the great problems of history and the fact that the perpetrators of evil and crimes against humanity sometimes go unpunished. Are these tremendous achievements, which generations will call wonders of the world, justified by the cruelty and harshness inherent in their creation?

We were contemplating the towering statue standing on its huge pedestal and saying whatever ideas came to our minds, while the boatman rowed slowly, not heeding what we were saying. One of us mentioned that de Lesseps had added his own private happiness to the opening ceremonies, being married again at sixty-four years of age. His new wife was a woman in the prime of her youth, twenty-one years old! The odd thing was that, by some magic, he sired eleven children before he died in old age. Thus, we thought, geniuses were distinguished in all things, even in their sexual prowess!

In those moments, we noticed that a motorboat was approaching us, on the side of which was written "Coast Guards" in Arabic and English. At first it passed us by; then we saw it turn around a few minutes later and head for us. One of the guards stood at the side parallel to our boat and blared through a megaphone in a colloquial Egyptian dialect, "O hajji! Who are those people with you?"

The boatman answered at the top of his voice, "They are Shamis, O Bey!"

"Shamis, meaning what?" came the question over the megaphone.

We helped our boatman by prompting him to say, "Arab students from Palestine."

So he repeated to the guard what we told him.

"You said, from Palestine?" the guard inquired, turning to one of his colleagues, apparently consulting him.

Then the motorboat came close to our boat, and this time, the guard specifically addressed us and in a clearly resolute tone, "Listen you! What are you doing here?"

The three of us answered together, "We are looking at de Lesseps for pleasure!"

"Fine! Please, come with us . . . and without objection!"

At first we did not understand what he meant, so he repeated the command. Minutes later and with difficulty—for we were mountain people and knew nothing about riding in boats or moving from one boat to another across the waves—we got into the coast guards' motorboat, bewildered by the situation. It was clear that they were arresting us because we were enjoying the sight of de Lesseps's statue and violating its sanctity.

Suddenly I remembered the boatman's fee, so I shouted, "Here are the ten piasters, hajji, with our thanks!"

And I threw the coin into his boat. He picked it up and waved goodbye to us. The motorboat took off at high speed to somewhere we did not know, and the three or four guards on it were silent, refusing to answer any of our questions as if they did not understand us or as if we were speaking the language of the people of Mars.

We landed at a place with many vessels and motorboats and were taken to a three-story building overlooking the sea; the words "Coast Guards" were also written on a big sign on its front.

Hamid said to me, "This is our just reward! You and Hilmi gave me a headache by ceaselessly speaking about de Lesseps . . . It seems they heard what we were saying, and they did not like it! Or else, they thought that we intended to blow up his statue. It is wartime, and the situation is complicated!"

We entered a large hall full of cigarette smoke. It had many desks at which sat men of all sorts and ages, most of them clearly tired or bored. They were reading newspapers and drinking coffee. We were taken to the upper floor, where there were more desks, men, newspapers, cups of coffee going back and forth, and cigarette smoke undulating in the air. We stood at a closed door, and here the guard who had been so active in arresting us

11

asked us to give him our passports. He then knocked on the door, leaving us behind as he entered and closed the door.

The nearest employee to us kindly said, "Please, people. Please, sit down."

We found some old chairs and sat down on them, almost overcome by incomprehension. What could they want from three Palestinian students leaving their homeland for the first time to seek learning in difficult circumstances like these?

Nobody spoke to us. The office attendants continued to carry trays with cups of coffee and glasses of water back and forth between the desks laden with piles of papers. The employees continued to read the newspapers or exchange jokes, no one of them paying any attention to us.

And we waited.

An hour or more passed, and the darkness before sunset began to fall on the sea that we could see through the windows. The employees turned on their electric lights, one after another, and we still waited for the magic door to open, through which the guard had disappeared with our passports.

Suddenly the door opened, and a policeman came out, but not the guard who had entered. Perhaps he was an officer, and he was holding the three brown passports. He approached us and by turn opened each passport and read aloud its owner's name, intently examining his face and the passport photograph.

Finally he said in a tender tone that we found to be strange, "Please, take your passports and go in peace."

When we stammered, objecting, and said, "But, sir, why did you . . . ?" He interrupted us as he shoved us in order to make us leave, saying, "Please, there is no need for any question. There has been a simple misunderstanding. I am sorry. Goodbye, goodbye!"

At his unexpected politeness, we realized that it was better for us not to seek any explanation . . . Each of us took his passport, put it in the inner pocket of his jacket, and left.

We left with some bitter feeling, for on the first day of our leaving our homeland (Palestine had hardly come out of the rebellion that had started in 1936 and had blazed until the declaration of the Second World War), our enthusiasm and our love for knowledge and our eagerness to see the visible traces of history led us nowhere but into the hands of the police! And God was our protector. We wondered, Where will this enthusiasm, this love, and this eagerness lead us in the coming days?

However, our bitterness did not last long. We wandered in the streets of Port Said, laughing at the ironic situation we had found ourselves in, for the people around us, wherever we turned, were good people. For two years or more, my greatest interest had been writing about experiencing life and knowing human beings. I thought, How can I acquire such experience and knowledge, having now started to go out into the big, wide world, if I am not prepared to be in ironic situations and contradictory ones, or in what could perhaps be much worse?

One of us said, "And what has been our individual share of misfortune when compared to experiences and contradictions, let alone the disappointments and frustrations, that fill the histories of all nations?"

Then we said, "At the end of the day, philosophy is a cause of hunger!"

Since we didn't have much money, we looked for a folksy restaurant and had a delicious supper of *kushari,* a dish made of spiced rice, lentils, and onions. Meanwhile, we continued to generously comment on everything we saw as if we were still viewing with pleasure the statue of Ferdinand de Lesseps!

2

Hamlet, Ophelia, and I

I spent my first academic year, from October 1939 to June 1940, at the University of Exeter in the south of England. Exeter is one of the most beautiful British cities. It lies on the slope of a mountain and descends into a wide valley in which the River Exe runs and ascends to a summit covered with the forest known as Stock

Woods. The city is thus endowed with various kinds of natural beauty in addition to possessing its roots in history, its ancient cathedral, its Royal College of Arts, and its important University College, which in those days was affiliated with the University of London. Furthermore, it is only a short distance from the sea, and being in the county of Devonshire, it is surrounded by some of the most beautiful countryside in England.

In those first nine months of my life in England, before I was twenty years old, all Exeter was the arena for my experiencing an expansion of intellectual and sensual freedom. I began to buy books almost daily and bought them wholesale, especially after I came to know a serious and sedate old man who loved books and who worked in one of the main bookstores of the city. He was responsible for the store's used books, which he bought from the large collections of people who had once collected them with love and care and whose heirs had then sold for the lowest prices. He used to let me in on valuable finds and lowered prices for me after he found out that, like him, I loved books, even their touch, their smell, and endless talk about them.

In Exeter I came to know male students like me with whom I enjoyed discussions and debates, and I came also to know female students who combined for me the joy of discussion and debate with the pleasure of beautiful friendship. This kind of friendship was mostly new to me, and it was not without a certain measure of flirtation, varying in the degree of innocence according to circumstances. In Exeter I learned to dance, imagining that the movements and rhythms of dance were a sort of a parallel to the movements and rhythms of thought. And I spent hours in the winter of that year on the mountain top covered with trees and snow, reciting crazy poetry in an English bejeweled with Arabic metaphors that fell like magic on the ears of this or that young woman as the sun gathered its red rays before sunset from the snow-covered horizons. The young women could not believe that their eyes or lips could excite such emotions and images in a young Arab man coming from the far hills of Jerusalem, for they had not found that their looks had ever such an effect on their male English friends. They did not know that I still carried in my heart the old, desert thirst.

Dolly's Café at eleven o'clock every morning, and especially on Saturdays, was the scene of many of those meetings full of surprises and innocent flirtatious intrigues. As music filled the air, I did not know who was ensnaring whom, the boy or the girl? I had an encounter with sixteen-year-old Bernadette, who used to skip school or church (for she was Catholic) so that we could meet. I imagined that she were the heroine of a short story entitled "Heaven's Daughter" that I had written in Jerusalem a year earlier, in which a charming young woman studied and lived in an old convent, intending to become a nun, and suddenly blossomed in my hands, with all life's terror . . . and ecstasy.

In Exeter I experienced love again. I had had an experience in Jerusalem that had remained platonic despite its pleasures and sleepless nights. This time, love was as stormy as a gale and as sweeping as a flood. Its space was the green fields and the high trees. It raged in the body as it did in the soul, for it was the soul that gave expression to it in indomitable and endless words.

At the University of Exeter, I was preparing myself to enter the University of Cambridge the following year to specialize in English literature. My concentration was to be on poets, especially modern ones, in addition to my two favorites, Shelley and Keats; and I also had a great interest in novelists. My wide-ranging interests made me very sensitive to the sound of words and the importance of metaphors, allusions, and symbols, something that had been a part of me since my school days at the Arab College. One of my teachers there, Jeffery Walton, had said in his report recommending me at the end of the academic year that I was "very widely read" compared to other students my age. His opinion surprised me, for I thought that varied and continual reading was one of the necessities of daily life.

Perhaps I was fortunate that Gladys Newby, the young girl of whom I was fond toward the end of that year's winter, was a student from the north of England. She was younger than I by a year or a little more. She studied Greek and Latin and knew by heart thousands of verses from English poetry and a lot about classical music; like me, she wanted to know more and to add to our intellectual enthusiasm much of the charm of Greek and Latin literature. She was surprised that, among the few things I had brought with me from Jerusalem, was an album of old records containing Beethoven's *Ninth Symphony*. Her long blond hair flowed down the sides of her face, which was always flushed with the fire of her emotions. I used to see her as the embodiment of a goddess in whom were blended the exuberance of Nordic adventurers from whom she may have descended and the warmth of the Mediterranean civilizations, which she studied out of love and which perhaps constituted some of the reasons why she was fond of me. I said to her once, "Do you know that the Mediterranean is mostly an Arab sea and that the legacy of the Greeks and the Romans blended with the Arab civilizations and spirit since their beginning? This is what has given permanence to all that is distinct and wonderful in this sea extending from the Canaanite Arab shore in the east to the Andalusian Arab shore in the west . . ." She discussed this idea with me for hours, as she did all others.

The war had not yet become severe in the first months, and so newspapers spoke of "the phony war." But the blackout prevailed and was strictly enforced. The city was drowned in darkness every night, which made going out to the streets at night fraught with awe and a special fascination. Then Germany stunned the countries of western Europe with her lightning attack, the blitzkrieg by which in a few days she was able to occupy a large part of western Europe and a large section of France after sweeping through the defenses of the Maginot line. The British armies suffered a terrible defeat, and their remnants were forced to rush to the port of Dunkirk on the northwestern shore of France, from which in vessels of all sorts and sizes rescued as many soldiers as possible, taking them by the thousands to ports in the south of England. One morning we saw battalions of exhausted soldiers who had been cast onto the shore by the waves marching in a great parade in the streets of Exeter and being welcomed by the masses and music. However, people began to fear for the first time that there might be a German surprise assault on England, the country that no enemy had dared to attack for over a thousand years.

However, university life continued to be the same, despite the fact that the number of young men was becoming fewer and fewer as they were called to military service. Our relationships and activities continued to grow despite the escalating severity and cruelty of the war's circumstances. The feeling of communal danger and impending disaster seemed to enhance our intellectual acuity and emotional agitation, redoubling our clinging to life and its feelings every day and every hour; that is, if death was inevitable. But death at any rate was to be resisted with this love for life, with this intensity of thought, and with this warmth of feeling. The result was that our activity increased at every level: in study, in work, in the arts. The air raids on cities by German bombers had not yet begun—that would start several months later, but without diminishing that mysterious lust for life.

■ ■ ■

At the beginning of summer, Gladys went back to her parents in the city of Hull in the north of Yorkshire. I went to Oxford to attend a course in English literature at Somerville College and was given a beautiful room for several weeks. At the end of the course, I chose to stay in Oxford to see its wonderful college buildings and rich libraries and repeatedly visit the poet Shelley's monument at New College, which represented him as a naked and drowning young man lamented by the goddess of poetry. Because of my meager funds, I stayed at a small hostel on a street near the railway station. All night I heard the hubbub of trains and their whistles as they entered the city and left it. I was often unable to sleep as I imagined what those ever-panting trains carried: people of all kinds and from all walks of life, luggage and merchandise and weapons, construction materials and destructive war materiel, commercial and business letters as well as letters of love and tragedy, among which were the letters I exchanged almost daily with Gladys, many of which contained my first, serious attempts at writing poetry in English.

I was finally informed that I had been admitted by the University of Cambridge as of the first week of October. That meant that I would definitely be separated from Gladys for the next few academic years. Around that time I received a strange but polite letter from a friend, Steve Dunkerly, who lived in Hull and who was studying at Exeter and was about to graduate. In the letter he said that he was fond of a young woman who loved me and that he wanted to marry her but she had turned him down because of me. He also said that he did not see how we could continue to sustain our relationship while she and I were at such a distance from each other, a distance which would continue to exist. However, when Gladys and I insisted that geographical distance would not change anything in our situation, the young man proved himself shortly afterwards by making a personal sacrifice for the sake of the happiness of the young woman he loved. And his proof was amazing . . .

Gladys and I were deprived of meeting each other in the months of that summer. My traveling north or her traveling south to meet was quite expensive, and neither my very meager budget nor hers could bear it. Furthermore, I was involved in my studies as well as in keeping up my artistic activities, attending plays, and writing poetry—which had begun to take most of my time.

The city of Stratford-upon-Avon, Shakespeare's birthplace, was near Oxford—one could go to and return from by train or bus on the same day—and was a constant lure for me. I once spent a wonderful day there and visited the house in which Shakespeare was born; and I tricked the attendant and committed the forbidden act of writing my name next to the poet Byron's on the wood frame of one of the windows. I roamed about in the city as one would in a holy place and visited many other places associated with the Bard, the greatest of the English people's poets. I also visited the Shakespeare Memorial Theatre built on the river dotted with the famous white swans swimming effortlessly as though in a dream continuing since the time Shakespeare wrote his sonnets and plays.

Hamlet was one of Shakespeare's plays I was especially interested in at that time. As it would for any other young man in conditions like mine, the play made me feel that I too carried with me the tragedies of my country wherever I went. Palestine was never out of my mind for a single moment, nor were my family's worries in that difficult period—and when were we Palestinians, ever since I was born, not passing through difficulties as individuals or as a nation? For it was as though we were trying daily to overpower a fate that never ceased to oppress us. Perhaps it gave me pleasure, as it did many other young men whom I came to know as the war escalated in its violence and destruction, to find ideas in some of Hamlet's situations and monologues that seemed to relate to me personally, as in his famous saying:

> To be, or not to be: that is the question.

This was the question with which I would fill the hearts of my students at the Rashidiyya College in Jerusalem, four or five years later.

Or when Hamlet says:

> How weary, stale, flat, and unprofitable,
> Seem to me all the uses of this world!
> [Fie on't! ah fie!] 'tis an unweeded garden,
> That grows to seed; things rank and gross in nature
> Possess it merely . . .

Or when he speaks to Yorick's skull, the king's jester in the past, when the gravedigger throws it at his feet so that he may meditate on the power of death over everything.

I felt that, despite everything, I might have to give up Gladys, the young woman who had finally come to personify love for me in its most colorful and tender forms, its most passionate emotions and pleasures, and its most beautiful and poetic fullness. I identified completely with the Prince of Denmark every time he spoke to himself or was alone with his beloved Ophelia. However, I tried to suppress these dark feelings by a sort of obstinacy that compelled me to take from life everything that excited my imagination and senses. Perhaps sorrow and joy were only the two faces of one single existential experience that I should capture and not forsake, one that I wanted to express in what I wrote, whatever the language I wrote in.

Toward the end of that summer, one of the big theatrical

troupes was presenting a season of Shakespeare in Stratford, eight plays every week at the Shakespeare Memorial Theatre—that is, a different play every evening from Monday through Saturday in addition to a matinee on Wednesday and Saturday. So I went to Stratford again, now as a pilgrim to see eight plays in one week. Every morning, I read the text of the play or plays I would see later in the day; the last of them, and crowning them all, was *Hamlet*. The copy of it that I read at the time remained among my books as a dear possession kept with a lover's sentiments.

It so happened that the week I went to Stratford was the last in the season, after which began ballet. So I stayed there to see the ballet performances beginning on Monday. Near the theater was a pub called the Dirty Duck, which was famous because, in addition to local residents, many of its patrons were actors. An Englishman and I had met there and become friends as we frequented it before or after the plays. On Monday evening, we were both at the pub, standing at the counter and holding glasses of beer, when a young man approached me with some hesitation, faltered as he greeted me with an undue politeness I did not know the reason for, and asked me, "Aren't you the famous ballet dancer in tomorrow's performance?"

I was amazed and said, "No. I'm sorry to disappoint you. But do you think I resemble the ballet dancer?"

He was perturbed and said, "Pardon me! Please excuse me!" He ordered a round of beer for all of us then departed. My friend said, "It's your slender face, your long hair, and your fingers with their . . ."

I interrupted him and whispered, "Don't turn back to look now. The ballerina is just behind you . . ."

At that moment, a young woman of about eighteen was entering the pub. She was tall and her hair was loose, and she wore a light, unbuttoned raincoat. She was in the company of her parents. She stood next to us, and her father ordered their drinks from the barman. That afternoon we had seen her in a tearoom, and she had aroused our interest as she entered with her distinct elegance, graceful bearing, and unusual beauty. We had thought her to be one of the ballet dancers at the time.

I looked at her over my friend's shoulder. She turned to me, turned away, then looked again at me deliberately and with some perplexity. When she was served her drink, she took it and went with her parents to a nearby table and sat down. I noticed that she continued to look at me, not paying attention to her parent's conversation. I became uneasy, standing there wondering, this beautiful woman coming from the wilds of the night in England—did she know me, or what?

Suddenly she rose to her feet and approached me with her svelte body and, in a serious tone tempered by a smile, she asked, "Are you Hamlet?"

I could not believe my ears, "Sorry! What did you say?"

"Are you Hamlet?" she repeated. "I mean, were you the one who played Hamlet yesterday?"

What do you say to a beautiful young woman, with black hair flowing down her shoulders and with lips resembling embers, when—either in jest or in earnest—she asks you "Are you Hamlet?"

I was filled with vanity and said, "Yes, I'm Hamlet. But I'm not playing his role . . . Are you the ballerina?"

She laughed, "Me? I wish I were!"

I said, "Will you allow me to offer you a drink?"

"Yes, please."

But before I asked what she wanted to drink, she turned to a nearby jukebox and said, still in an embarrassed but assured tone, "Will you choose a record for me?" And she opened her handbag to look for a coin to slide into the jukebox.

I said, "No. You choose and I'll pay."

I put a coin into the slot, and she pressed a button, near which was written, "I love you more, more than I should."

She uttered a sweet, cunning laugh and ran to her table to fetch her glass. A few moments later, she introduced us to her parents. I then left my friend with her parents to talk to them about his job in London, and Jane Harrison and I went into the Shakespearean darkness outdoors. I stopped her on the sidewalk and asked, "Why did you ask me if I was Hamlet?"

"Don't you know?" she asked. Then she added, "Because that

was a way to start a conversation with you . . . In fact, I saw you yesterday among the audience in the theater."

I said, "Then you are Ophelia! In your prayers, mention all my sins!"

I took her by the arm and led her on as she said, "But I don't want to die by drowning . . ."

"You'd rather live," I answered, "and restore to Hamlet some sanity."

She said, "I'd rather want more madness for him . . . just like me."

And we spent several days in Shakespearean woods full of exploding suns until she returned to her home in Birmingham, and I to my room in Oxford.

■ ■ ■

There, I found three letters from Gladys waiting for me. In the last one, she said that she could no longer control her patience and that we should meet as soon as possible and in any place I wanted. I was overjoyed by her sudden decision, for I was worried that the new Ophelia would distract me from the woman whose words, even when in a letter, still kindled fires in my heart.

I wrote her a long letter and mentioned, though briefly and cautiously, my meeting Jane Harrison, and I suggested that we meet in Stratford, for that would shorten the way for her somewhat, and we could stay at the hostel, for its owners had come to know me by then.

Four or five days later, she responded in a telegram in which she said, "Arriving Stratford Saturday afternoon. Please reserve three rooms. With my love."

Three rooms? I thought there was a typo in the telegram. I could understand that we might need two rooms, one for her and one for me. But a third room? At any rate, I wired the hostel in Stratford and reserved three rooms. On Saturday I went to Stratford, and there was the surprise.

The September weather had begun to change, and Saturday was as rainy and stormy as a winter day, the kind of day—as is usual in England—nature spitefully brings before the end of summer.

After lunch I kept looking out of the window from time to time, not knowing exactly how and when Gladys would arrive. In moments when the rain stopped, I went out to the street and walked on the sidewalk lined with trees, my nerves worn by waiting and expectation.

I walked for a long distance; then I thought of returning lest Gladys arrive at the hostel and not find me there waiting for her. Suddenly I saw a man at a distance riding a motorcycle and speeding toward me. He wore a helmet, goggles, and leather gloves. Behind him sat a young woman with both her arms around him for fear of falling. She wore trousers, goggles, and leather gloves like his. Her long hair flew in the strong wind, although most of it was covered by a silk scarf she had tied under her chin. As the two riders came nearer to me, the man reduced his speed and stopped his roaring motorcycle along the sidewalk next to me.

Gladys jumped off the back seat, took off her goggles, and threw herself into my arms with her drenched raincoat. Her lips were like two halves of a cold, moist fruit, melting but not dissolving on my lips.

As for the man, he was no other than Steve Dunkerly who wanted to marry her. He got off his motorcycle, waited until Gladys and I had finished embracing and had finally caught our breath; he took off his gloves and shook hands with me warmly. Then he said, "I'll precede you to the hostel . . ." He returned to his motorcycle and rode it in the direction I pointed, while Gladys and I returned on foot.

Steve had volunteered to bring Gladys on his motorcycle, covering a distance of about four hundred kilometers. They had begun their trip at the crack of dawn and traveled in the rain and wind so that Gladys might have the chance of seeing me in the city I loved . . .

What happened in the remaining part of that day and the night following is not possible to narrate easily, for it was like a dream: some of it was terror, and most of it was pleasure, but all of it was like something impossible.

There was no place for Ophelia in those hours crowded with feelings and words that came from a tempest worthy of characters whom, I felt, no one but Shakespeare could create so well. I was increasingly under the illusion that, in all we said and did, we were moving as though in one of his plays. I was hoping it might be a comedy. But who knows when events will change at the whim of the goddess of fate, or when her wheel will turn to bring a tragedy about? For tragedy in reality, as in poetry, lurks for us around the corner of every road on which we walk unaware of what is coming.

3

The Lady of the Lakes

The Lake District was the first place I thought of traveling to for the spring break of 1940, having earlier spent the winter break in London. I wanted to go there not only because the Lake District is one of the most beautiful areas of England but because it was the place in which the Romantic movement started at the beginning of the nineteenth century. William Wordsworth and Samuel Coleridge were two of the leading poets of this movement, and they lived in that district for an important part of their lives and wrote there much that was inspired by its "generous skies." The two other Romantic poets influenced by them were Percy Bysshe Shelley and John Keats, both younger than they. I in turn was still under the influence of their deep magic that had affected me since my final academic year at the Arab College in 1938. Then my interest widened to include all the Lake Poets, as English literary history calls them, and all the details of the Romantic movement itself with its many names. In my first months at the University of Exeter, I read a lot of works by the Lake Poets and about them, as well as about the places that had inspired them; and the names of those lakes and their surroundings had become familiar. I imagined that I would have no need of a map of the Lake District if I wanted to go to Windermere, Hawkshead, Ambleside, Grasmere, or Derwent Water.

As soon as I settled in a small hotel in Windermere, by the lake of the same name, and made it my base for my daily tours, my mind teemed with images, feelings, and memories. Some of them went back to my childhood, rich with the experience of nature in its primal forms: the soil and the rocks, the valley and the mountain, the trees and the wild flowers, the red anemones and the thorns, the wide blue skies and the downpours of rain, plunging in the mud and surrendering to the wind and thunder . . . Other images, feelings, and memories went back to my reading of the poetry of Wordsworth himself in Jerusalem a year earlier. I read him while going back and forth from our home, situated in a lowland crowded with houses and people, to the fields near our neighborhood where the town suddenly ended and where sparse olive trees, grass, and wild plants had absolute mastery. I used to be totally engrossed in Wordsworth's poetry, which made mystical one's experience of nature and the simple people living in its lap, uniting man with nature, and both with the Godhead.

I began roaming the winding paths between the hills of the Lake District and its villages. In my raincoat pockets, I carried works by Wordsworth and Coleridge, and I referred to them whenever I stopped to rest. I did not forget this time to carry my Kodak camera with me. It was the one which my brother Yousuf had given me as a present just before I left the homeland; it was the bellows type common in the 1930s. You opened it when you used it; then as you pushed the extended apparatus back, its pleats folded and it closed. It did not take much space when put in its leather case or, if you wished, in your raincoat pocket along with a book.

Since the first step of my tour, I recalled Wordsworth's visions that he had so beautifully created in *The Prelude,* in his ode, "Intimations of Immortality," and in his sonnets, in which he celebrated distancing oneself from the city and its universe, where "we lay waste our powers," in preference to scenes of the sea or fields where

> The winds that will be howling at all hours,
> And are up-gathered now like sleeping flowers

He remembered his childhood

>   when like a roe
> I bounded o'er the mountains, by the sides
> Of the deep rivers, and the lonely streams,
> Wherever nature led. . . .
>
> . . . .
>   The sounding cataract
> Haunted me like a passion; the tall rock,
> The mountain, and the deep and gloomy wood,
> Their colors and their forms were then to me
> An appetite; a feeling and a love,
> That had no need of a remoter charm
>
> . . . .
> Unborrowed from the eye.

I visited first the village of Grasmere in order to visit the house in which Wordsworth had spent productive years of his life with his sister Dorothy and his friend Coleridge, who published with him a collection of poems entitled *Lyrical Ballads,* which included the "Preface" written by Wordsworth and which is considered to be the manifesto of the new Romantic poetry. That evening, I reread Coleridge's narrative poem, "Christabel," and I recalled the extraordinary mysterious ambiguity that the young Coleridge was capable of inspiring through his poetry, something he had already demonstrated in his long poem "The Ancient Mariner." He realized it again in the story of Christabel, who one night finds the young breathtaking beauty Geraldine in a remote place where she had been attacked and abandoned by someone unknown. Christabel takes her to her father's castle, where this Geraldine, who is really a dreadful enchantress, casts a spell on her that cannot be explained even by madness.

That evening too, I wrote a letter to Gladys Newby and told

her about my pleasant and complex fascination with the unparalleled natural beauty of the place and the poetry that filled me with its charm as though it were a flooding river carrying me on waves of ecstasy that I was unable to speak of in a rational way. I also wrote a letter to my brother Yousuf in Jerusalem, claiming that God had created two paradises, one in Heaven for His good servants and the other on earth, called the Lake District, for those who loved nature.

Just before noon on my third day there, my tour took me to Scafell Pike, that famous mountain on the edge of the hills and the blue lakes embraced by them. It was another area that had inspired many poets and writers. It is more than three thousand feet high; clouds abide on its summit and lightning suddenly flashes on its crest, followed by thunder whose echo reverberates from hill to hill until it dies in the distance. On that day, it appeared like a joyful and playful jester under a clear sky and an abundant and tender sun with no heat. A cold refreshing breeze blew from time to time, carrying the aroma of wild plants and early spring flowers. I was walking on a rocky path that countless feet had smoothed over the centuries. I was going toward a curve, from which I would begin ascending the mountain. At that moment and although there were many people walking in that area, I found myself to be alone and unable to see anyone for a long distance in front of me or anywhere around me.

Suddenly a woman appeared from around the curve and walked toward me on the rocky path. I immediately noticed her long white dress, which was unusual for that place, its length billowing around her legs. A small, red bag hung from her shoulder. I thought she was not merely a tourist like me but rather a poet who had perhaps seized the opportunity of the bright sunshine and come to seek inspiration from the mountain's rocks and the blue lakes. I liked her long black hair flowing on her shoulders, or rather being blown by the wind that made it fly around her face and divide into locks on her chest. She made no effort to rearrange it, but her face shone now and then when the locks of her hair rose to uncover her cheeks before settling again on her shoulders. Perhaps she was descending from the mountain top toward which I was ascending with my old camera and more than one collection of poetry in the pockets of my raincoat.

The woman kept coming closer to me and I to her, but although we were the only two human beings in that remote area drowned in sunshine and buffeted by the wind, I was not one to try even to greet her. But she was bolder than I, directing her steps exactly toward me and looking at me expressly so that I had to avoid her lest we collide.

But what stranger would not welcome another stranger in a strange land like that? If the other stranger was a woman who had loose black hair flowing over a long white dress and green eyes that shone in her glowing face and sent rays to my eyes and who stood face to face with me, had I any choice to do anything but stop and say to her, "Hello . . . Good morning"?

When she returned my greeting, my amazement at her beauty grew: she was perhaps twenty-five years of age, or a little older. What was a young woman with that beauty, those green eyes, and that abundant tousled hair doing in a place like this all by herself? She did not smile when I said to her, with no intention other than to start a conversation, "Have you lost your way? Do you know where you're going?"

She answered, "I've lost my way and this is not the first time. How about you? Do you know where you're going?"

I said, "Yes, I want to go up to the top of this mountain."

She fell silent and glared at me with her green eyes, then she asked, "Are you a stranger here?"

I said, "Yes, a stranger, like you."

She said, "I meant whether you are from another country. You're not an Englishman, are you?"

My accent had given me away, for I had not spent more than six or seven months in England.

I said, "Yes, I'm from another country."

Her face showed greater interest in me, and I even imagined that she was pleased that I was not from her country.

She asked, "What country are you from?"

And before I replied, she added, "Let me guess . . . You're Spanish."

"No."

"Greek, then."

"No . . . I'm a Palestinian."

I was surprised to see her amazement, and she exclaimed, "No! That's impossible!"

I said, "I'm from Jerusalem."

She came closer to me and raised her hand as if to touch my chest, still amazed. "My God!" she said. "Are you really from the place on whose roads He walked? From the place in which He spoke, suffered, and was crucified?"

I had not expected that kind of question and thought she might be somewhat religious. And how easy it is for surroundings like those to arouse a sense of the hidden connections between a person and his or her Creator?

I said, "Yes, ma'am. And if the matter interests you . . ."

I refrained from expressing the rest of what I intended to say, being aware that I might exaggerate and unfairly take advantage of the situation.

She placed her palm on my chest and a strange hope shone in her green eyes as she said, "Yes, I'm interested . . ."

So I said, "And I spent all the years of my childhood a few steps from the grotto in which He was born . . ."

"In Bethlehem?"

"In Bethlehem."

She clasped her hands like one praying and whispered as though she feared hearing what she wanted to hear, "And you speak His language?"

I said, "I speak Arabic, the language that is nearest to the language He spoke . . ."

She said, "My God! Arabic? Aramaic?"

I said, "Yes, and Aramaic, some of which I learned at school in my childhood."

She raised her large eyes to heaven, while the wind still blew her hair around her face and blew my own long hair too—for she had distracted me from straightening it—and she exclaimed, "O my God! O my God!"

At this juncture, I felt embarrassed. What should I do or say in that situation, with a woman whom I imagined at first to be a poet and who, lo and behold, was now teetering on the verge of a "divine" rapture with which I was not familiar? I wanted to change the course of the conversation and come back to reality, so I asked her, "Have you gone up this mountain?"

But she persisted in her ecstasy, ignored my question, and said, "He always said, 'I am the Way . . .' Please, let me hear this expression in Aramaic."

Fortunately, that was an expression I knew, so I said it as she wanted.

She joined her hands again as though in warm, fervent prayer and exclaimed as her green eyes were now fixed on mine, "O my God! And do you know anything from His sermon on the mount?"

I laughed and said, "Sorry, ma'am. It's been too long, and I'm now immersed in the poetry of Wordsworth, Coleridge, and John Keats."

Once again, she refused to change the topic of our conversation and repeated, "Tell me in the language of Jesus, 'Blessed are the poor for they shall inherit the earth.'"

Here, I had no way to dodge her request, and I said in Arabic, enunciating every word as best I could, "Blessed . . . are the poor . . . for they . . . shall inherit . . . the earth."

"How beautiful these words are!" she said and turned around as the wind blew more strongly and made her long white dress flutter like wings. Then she brushed the hair from her eyes as if she wanted to be sure she could see me clearly and said, "And how did He say in that beautiful language, 'Come unto me, all ye that labour and are heavy laden, and I will give you rest . . .'?"

I don't deny that, at that moment, I wished I could have held her close to my chest, shut her eyes with two kisses, and whispered in her own language the comforting expression she wanted to hear, for she was undoubtedly heavy laden, very heavy laden. But I kept my composure and uttered the expression in Arabic in my own way, enunciating as before, "Come unto me, . . . all ye that labour . . . and are heavy laden . . . and I will . . . give you rest . . ."

I noticed that she was looking attentively at my lips as I uttered the words. She then surprised me by touching my lips with the fingers of her right hand, then passing them over my cheek and raising them to my eyes as though to ascertain that I was real, not a delusion or hallucination. All the while, she repeated, "O my God, O my God . . ."

When I raised my hand to hold her fingers roaming my face, she pulled them gently away and began to feel my shoulders, my neck, and my chest with both hands . . . Then she took a step backward and continued to withdraw down the path while still facing me, her hands raised with open fingers, and she walked backward, not afraid of stumbling over the stones.

As for me, I stayed frozen in place, breathless and terrified at the same time, looking at her as she backed farther and farther away from me while the wind blew around us, buffeting her until she disappeared around the curve and I could see her no longer.

I shook my head violently to expel my puzzlement. I turned uphill again and walked a few steps. But I remained possessed by her image and voice, unable to shake them off. It occurred to me to follow her, but I was afraid to know more about her. I repeated her expression, "O my God, O my God . . ." Did she think I was a vision that had appeared to her, even though she touched my face and my chest with her hand, but remaining unconvinced of what she touched. But wanting to preserve the experience of her vision, she avoided any other physical contact with me lest she should lose the ecstasy of her vision? Was I a holy illusion that suddenly embodied itself to her, so she left before it left her?

All of a sudden, I remembered the camera and took it out of my raincoat pocket, turned on my heel, and ran in the direction in which she had withdrawn. I reached the curve, panting and expecting to see her sitting on a rock, perhaps waiting for me, so I could then take a picture or two of her in that aroused state.

O my God! I saw no one.

The rugged path was empty, and the wind raised thin clouds of dust. Where did she go, how could she disappear? Did she go up that rocky cleft to the mountain top? So fast? Impossible! Was I a vision to her, or was she a vision that appeared to my eyes in that atmosphere charged with the poems I had read, then disappeared? Was I the victim of an unexpected hallucination?

I quickly withdrew and returned to walk uphill, not wanting to abandon my puzzlement this time. I began to feel deeply relieved that the lady of the lakes had not been waiting for me. I remembered Christabel and the sorceress Geraldine. I remembered the story of "La Belle Dame sans Merci," the beautiful lady without mercy whom Keats portrayed as roaming green meadows, with her long hair and unearthly singing. She met a knight errant who carried her on his steed, and she took him to her elfin grot where she sighed in agony and wept, and he shut her wild eyes with four kisses. She lulled him until he was overcome by sleep, and he dreamed of kings, princes, and knights who, tormented by ardent love, writhed with pain and were emaciated and pale like the dead. They shouted to him,

> "La Belle Dame sans Merci
> Hath thee in thrall!"

When he woke up, he found himself alone and wandered aimlessly about, the roses on his cheeks having withered, and his brow having become as pale as lilies . . .

I hit my forehead with my fist, angry at myself, "Why didn't I take out my camera as soon as I met her? Why didn't I take a picture of her as she talked with me and when she was leaving me with her wonderful face turned toward me? Who will believe me when I tell the story of what I saw, having no evidence in hand to prove it?"

However, I persuaded myself that I would inevitably see her on the mountain top, for she ascended to it through that rocky cleft. Inevitably . . .

I spent the rest of the day going up the mountain. When I reached the top, I saw many people there and asked some of them to take pictures of me with my camera. From the summit, I looked down in all directions and saw men and women ascending and descending the mountain's slopes. As for the lady of the lakes with the long white dress and the loose black hair flowing in the wind, I could not see her wherever I looked. The day ended, and I found no trace of her.

And I have not forgotten her, to this day.

4

My Story with Agatha Christie

Toward the end of September 1948, after the first *nakba* (catastrophe) of Palestine had come to a head, I was officially assigned to teach at the higher institutes (that is, the university colleges) in Iraq. I left my family in Bethlehem and went to Baghdad. In my suitcases I had a few items of clothing, many books and papers, and a number of oil paintings that I had done on relatively small pieces of plywood because they were easy to carry from place to place.

I was appointed a lecturer in English literature at the Preparatory College, which had just been established and which was described as the nucleus of the University of Baghdad that was to be established at that time. I was given a room to live in at the college, which was located in a large modern building at al-Azamiyya, near Antar Square, that later became the College of Sciences. I was one of three Palestinian professors given rooms in the building in return for certain supervisory duties in the boarding section. We were in charge of about one hundred students from all parts of Iraq, who had been chosen because they ranked first in their high schools. We were to prepare them educationally and culturally to be sent on scholarship to European and American universities.

My two colleagues were the poet Mahmoud al-Hout and the linguist Fahd al-Rimawi. The Palestinian historian Zuhdi Jarallah was also a lecturer, in addition to four English professors, the most prominent personality of whom was Desmond Stewart, who had come to Baghdad immediately after graduating from the University of Oxford in the classics. He was twenty-four years old and, like us, wrote prose and poetry and sought a literary reputation. Because of the intimate friendship that arose between him and us that year and the following years, he became interested in the cause of Palestine* and subsequently in other Arab causes. He later dedicated most of his time to this interest, learned Arabic, wrote a lot, and achieved wide fame in England and America as a novelist and an expert on Arab causes. He supported these causes passionately and intelligently in all that he wrote in the following years of his life.

On one of the first days after taking up residence at the college, I was at the Mackenzie Bookstore talking to its owner Karim, a very kind Iraqi who had inherited the bookstore from its original English owners because he had worked with them in managing it since it had been established before the Second World War and had become knowledgeable about new foreign books. To that he added his experience in dealing with Arabic books, both classical and modern Iraqi ones. His bookstore on al-Rashid Street, the most important street in Baghdad in those days, was the meeting place of many Iraqi and foreign intellectuals. They all had a personal relationship with him, and he carefully tried to meet all their book needs. He kept the name Mackenzie Bookstore because the name was famous and familiar, so much so that he himself came to be known as Karim Mackenzie in a manner of speaking, and his bookstore remained one of the landmarks of the city.

I raised my eyes from the book I was leafing through and saw a man next to me reaching for another book and looking at me at the same time, questioningly.

"Robert!" I exclaimed.

"Jabra!" he responded.

---

*In the introduction to his book, *The Palestinians: Victims of Expediency,* Desmond Stewart says that I was the person who filled his mind and feelings with the Palestinian cause from the very moment of his arrival in Baghdad in 1948 as a lecturer. He continued to write about it and to be inspired by it until the end of his life. To be noted is the fact that this book was the last thing he wrote, and it was published after his death in 1981.

34

"What are you doing here?"

"What are you yourself doing here?"

"I teach at a college here."

"And I work in archaeology."

The questions and answers continued between us. Robert Hamilton was an archaeologist who, for a number of years, had been the director of the Rockefeller Museum for Palestinian Antiquities in Jerusalem, where we often saw each other. Fondness for Palestinian antiquities and ancient history had brought us together and also a love of music and art, especially sculpture or what little was available in the Jerusalem museum situated outside the city walls in the vicinity of Herod's Gate near the Rashidiyya College, where I had taught for more than four years before going to Baghdad. It appeared that he had left Jerusalem early in 1948 and joined the British Archaeological Expedition in Baghdad, which was an institution going back to the early 1920s. Among its prominent personalities was Sir Charles Leonard Woolley* who "discovered" in southern Iraq the city of Ur, or rather the royal cemetery in it. The excavations had continued from the middle 1920s to the middle 1930s and had unearthed relics that were among the most amazing ever discovered in the world, including the remains of the wonderful Queen Shebad and her many maidservants in their marvelous jewelry. Woolley wrote a famous book entitled *Ur of the Chaldees* about his excavations and attracted the world's attention to that ancient city, deeply rooted in the history of human civilization.

Hamilton said, "Do you know Max Mallowan?"

I said, "No."

He said, "You should get to know him, he is an extraordinary personality. Perhaps you don't know much about Iraqi antiquities. Max Mallowan is rediscovering Nimrud, and I work with him."

I asked him about Nimrud, and he said, "At one time, it was the capital of the Assyrians in the north. Its ancient name was Calah . . . It's a place like no other. Come and visit us there."

---

*Jabra's text mistakenly mentions him as Sir Arthur Woolley. *(Translator's note.)*

I said, "I wish I could! I'm new here, and preoccupied with getting accustomed to Baghdad."

He said, "Listen, we are having dinner tomorrow at Mallowan's home. Why don't you join us for dinner? I'll tell Mrs. Mallowan today. And we'll talk a lot about Nimrud . . ."

When I accepted his invitation, I asked, "And where is the house?"

He said, "It's the house of King Ali. Do you know it? It is in the Karradat Maryam neighborhood, right on the riverbank. It's an old Turkish house that goes back to the Ottoman period, and it is one of the most beautiful homes of old Baghdad."

I gave him a slip of paper, and he drew a map on it to help me reach this house situated on the opposite bank of the Tigris River. For some time in the 1920s it was the residence of King Ali, brother of King Faysal I, and he named the house after himself, being a king without a kingdom.

At eight o'clock, the following evening, I entered the gate of the house and walked into an open space of characteristic Ottoman Baghdadi style, surrounded by trees and flowers. In the middle was a two-story building: one ascended to the upper story by a flight of external wooden stairs leading to a long narrow balcony extending all along the house front with the doors of the rooms opening onto it. One of these doors was open and lit for arriving visitors.

I went up the wooden stairs, on every step of which was a flowerpot. A man of medium height, forty years old, came out to meet me. He was lively and clearly intelligent.

"Mr. Jabra, right?" he immediately said. "I'm Max Mallowan."

He pulled me inside by the hand in order to introduce me to the lady of the house, Mrs. Mallowan. In turn she shook hands with me and introduced me to two other men in the room.

She said, "Mr. Robert Hamilton, whom you know. I'm pleased that he invited you to come this evening . . . And Mr. Seton Lloyd, consultant at the Department of Iraqi Antiquities."

When I shook his hand, a little surprised, I asked him, "Are you the husband of the sculptor Heidi Lloyd?"

He replied, "Strange! Do you know her?"

I said, "I met her more than three years ago in Jerusalem, and I haven't forgotten her. She told me that she was teaching sculpture in Baghdad and that her husband was an archaeologist . . ."

While Mrs. Mallowan was looking at us with a smile as though waiting for us to complete our introductory small talk, he said, "It's indeed a small world! Heidi spoke to me about you when she returned from Jerusalem at the time, and she said you wrote poetry . . . and you painted. Is that right? I'm sorry I did not know that you were the person when Robert mentioned your name to me. But who ever thought we would meet here, in Baghdad!"

"And where is Mrs. Lloyd?" I asked.

He said, "She's in London at present. She hasn't taught at the Institute of Fine Arts for some time now."

Mrs. Mallowan asked me as she led me to my seat, "And what brought you to Baghdad?"

"An old love," I said briefly, "and our tragedy in Palestine."

"Oh, yes, yes . . . Come and tell us. At least you're an eyewitness . . ."

Max Mallowan asked what I would like to drink and then brought me the glass as his wife returned to her comfortable seat and put on the tip of her nose the eyeglasses that had hung on a chain around her neck. She picked up a skein of wool and her knitting and began working on it with her needles as soon as she sat down. Once again she said, "Yes, do tell us. What exactly happened to our dear Jerusalem?"

It seemed to me she was in her late fifties, somewhat plump and well built. Her face was broad, and she was self-confident and had the humility of a generous hostess. Our conversation about Palestine was quite long, and I concentrated on the Zionist acts of killing, eviction, and land usurpation; and the fine lady repeated as she knitted her yarn, "All this must be known to the world . . . And in detail . . . Writers must write about these atrocities, about this inhumanity that, we used to say, the Second World War would put an end to . . . We wanted that war to end all wars—but it seems that we have started again to sow the seeds of many future wars. The British Empire shouldn't come to an end like this . . ."

This fine lady did not know that my colleague Desmond Stewart and I, in association with Haydar al-Rikabi, broadcast regular talks in English at night from Baghdad's radio station about these tragedies, and that we called upon the conscience of the world and cried out to everyone who had a conscience to listen and say a word of truth supporting us.

We also talked about the historical relations of Palestine and Iraq from ancient times, and they told me about their continuing excavations in Nimrud. I learned that Seton Lloyd had written a book entitled *Twin Rivers: A Brief History of Iraq from the Earliest Times to the Present Day,* which had been translated into Arabic a few years earlier, and another famous book about Iraq entitled *Foundations in the Dust: A Story of Mesopotamian Exploration,* of which I later bought a copy from the Mackenzie Bookstore and learned a lot from it about the successive ancient civilizations of Mesopotamia. It became clear to me, however, that Lloyd was about to leave for another archaeological position in Ankara after having spent twenty eventful years full of discoveries in Iraq.

I found out that the three archaeologists, with whom Mrs. Mallowan kept my conversation continuous and enjoyable, were all authors of archaeological research articles that had been published in England and some in *Sumer,* the journal published by the Department of Antiquities in Baghdad. Having reached the twenty-ninth year of my life, I felt at that moment that I had been struggling since adolescence with that terrible fever, the fever of writing. I had written nothing but two novellas that I had not published; a few short stories, some of which I had not yet completed; much poetry, most of which I kept to myself; in addition to a number of essays, some of which I had broadcast by radio and published in recent months but did not like very much. When we began our dinner, I thought to myself that the only person in the room who was not suffering from the fever of writing and did not know its agonies and pains, other than the servant who brought our dishes with great respect, was Mrs. Mallowan. She had nothing to do but raise ideas for discussion about contemporary and ancient events and about human nature. It was sufficient for her to knit a pullover for her husband (who was definitely younger than she was) that would protect him from the cold when exposed to the harsh vagaries of nature as he extracted, with the obstinacy of a lover, history's evidence and hidden mysteries from the depths of the hills in the north, those barren hills that concealed in their interiors obscure relics of man's achievements, of which most often nothing remained to us, not even the merest suggestion.

They were all, including Mrs. Mallowan, about to leave for Mosul to resume their excavation in Nimrud and continue the archaeological digs that Henry Layard had begun in 1845, more than one hundred years earlier, thinking incorrectly that Nimrud was Nineveh and surprising the world in those days with the wonders of sculpture and facts of history he discovered.

■ ■ ■

I later saw Max Mallowan and his wife once or twice on public occasions, and I noticed how alert Mrs. Mallowan was to all that happened around her and to all the people she saw.

In May of 1949, a play in English was performed in King Faysal II's Hall (now the People's Hall). On such occasions you would see around you most of the intellectuals of Baghdad, both Iraqis and foreigners, because the city had not yet grown very much in size or population. One felt that one knew everyone who deserved to be known in the city and that, in return, one was known to them all. College professors and graduates, few as they were in comparison with the number twenty years later, used to come together in large numbers on cultural occasions, such as public lectures, art exhibits (although rare), concerts of classical music given by the new Iraqi Symphony Orchestra, or plays, especially those performed by visiting companies.

During the intermission, I went out with a friend to the refreshments hall like other spectators. Lo and behold, we were face to face with Mallowan and his wife drinking coffee (Pepsi and Coca-Cola had not yet entered Iraq). We commented in a light manner on the acting we had seen and asked about a point or two. When I returned to the counter to leave my coffee cup,

Desmond Stewart saw me and asked jokingly, "Have you found a solution to the crime?"

I did not understand what he meant and asked, "What crime?"

He replied, "The crime invented by the lady, whom I saw you talking to."

"Sorry, I still don't understand what you mean."

"Have you not been talking to Agatha Christie?"

His question surprised me, and I thought he was still joking. I said in all simplicity, "I have been talking to Max Mallowan and his wife."

"I thought you knew!" he exclaimed. "Mrs. Mallowan is the mystery writer Agatha Christie."

"Impossible!"

"Go back to her and assure yourself."

But the intermission was coming to an end, and the spectators were going back into the theater. I returned to my seat, not believing what I had just heard. Was this really Agatha Christie, whose mysteries and detective novels I had read since my youth? How was it that I visited and discussed matters with her without thinking for a moment that she ever held a pen in her hand to write? I could not follow the second half of the play in expectation of its end, and it seemed as though it would never end. When the curtain finally came down and the people began to leave their seats after the applause, I left my friend and hurried through the crowd and looked for Mrs. Mallowan until I caught sight of her standing with her husband at the outside door waiting for their car. I went to her and asked her directly, "Are you really Agatha Christie?"

The fine lady laughed and simply answered, "Yes."

I said, "I'm sorry I didn't know that."

She said, "Better, better! When will you visit us in Nimrud?"

■ ■ ■

I later learned that the author of the famous mysteries and detective novels had retained the name she had acquired before the 1920s from her first husband, Colonel (Archibald) Christie.

After he left her and died, she had become so famous under that name that she did not want to abandon it whenever she published yet another of her novels, which followed one other with regularity and rapidity and which were translated into many other languages and earned her large royalties. When she married the archaeologist Max Mallowan after meeting him in Iraq, specifically at Ur, she began to accompany him to the countries of the Arab East where he worked; and it was said that she spent her own private wealth on some of his archaeological projects. She made some of her experiences on these trips the background of a number of exciting "crimes" in her novels, whose mysteries were solved from time to time by the Belgian inspector Hercule Poirot, the character she first created in 1920—as in *Murder on the Orient Express* (1934), *Death on the Nile* (1937), and others.

The seasons she spent with her husband in Iraq for many years usually began toward the end of winter and ended three or four months later in the middle of spring. She normally did not stay long in Baghdad but preferred to be at the sites of the excavations, near their mounds and heaps of earth, and among the workers and researchers and the archaeological finds that they came upon from time to time. There she wrote, having isolated herself in an unexpected and extraordinary manner from the contemporary city and its life in order to live in the milieu of the settings, the characters, and relationships that her imagination created far away from the place, the time, and the people surrounding her. Her novelistic universe remained that of the 1920s—or rather a specific form of it—and she refused to change anything in it despite the sweeping changes that society and manners had undergone in London and other capitals of the world in the 1930s and the following decades. That universe served her creative impulse, a persistent imaginative need, from which she could make an absolutely delightful and exciting intellectual recreation for millions of people.

In those days I had read two of her novels, the events of which take place in Iraq, namely *Murder in Mesopotamia* and *They Came to Baghdad*. I found that the atmosphere and the characters of both did not differ much from those of her novels set in England, except for her description of the markets of Basra in one and of the Zia Hotel and its owner in Baghdad in the other. She made no claim to be concerned with social, political, or documentary matters. It was rather the clever crime plot that required that she move her characters within the confines of her basic intellectual creation. No importance is thus attached to the surroundings of the event other than the undefined background it offers to this game, which is almost purely mathematical in its logic and construction. Desmond Stewart did exactly the opposite in the 1950s and thereafter in his novels that are set in Iraq, later in Lebanon, and finally in Egypt and also in the very different settings of his trilogy, the family saga entitled *Succession of Roles*.

Two years later, on March, 22, 1951, to be exact, I finally had the opportunity to visit Nimrud / Calah, the capital of the Assyrians during one of their great periods in the ninth and eighth centuries BC. It had been established four centuries before that, and the Medians were the ones who finally put an end to it by destroying and burning it in 612 BC when Nineveh, the next capital of the Assyrians fell at the hands of the Babylonian leader Nabopolassar, father of King Nebuchadnezzar. The Nimrud / Calah civilization lasted for about six hundred years.

I still remember the exact date of the visit because it was the second day after the beginning of spring, and the day became associated in my memory with a deeply felt emotion upon seeing the remains of one of the most wonderful of the ancient Arab civilizations, as far as art and culture were concerned. My guide and companion in that lovely region of Iraq was my friend, Zayd Ahmad Uthman. Bonds of affection had grown between us after being introduced in 1950 by the poet Buland al-Haydari and Zayd's younger brother Mahmoud. Zayd wanted me to see the north in his company, for he knew every corner of it, every town and village, as a knowledgeable citizen who loved his homeland. He was one of the young deputies in the National Assembly, and his father, before him, had been a prominent figure among the Kurds, mayor of Arbil, and member of the Senate. I felt that Zayd Ahmad Uthman was following in his father's footsteps while possessing a thirst for knowledge and modernity.

When we reached the site of the excavations, Robert Hamilton received us warmly and seemed to be in a strange state of excitement and joy. I immediately remarked that he was not his usual self. "Of course not," he said as he led us to the dig. "This morning we discovered a magnificent stela . . . It is a picture of Shalmaneser III, standing in his full height . . . Here it is. Look! A work of art, a very precious work of art . . . Do you see these symbols? This writing? . . ."

Shalmaneser III was the son of Ashurnasirpal II, the great conqueror, who transferred his capital from Ashur to Nimrud in the ninth century BC. He was the first to immortalize his deeds with murals of relief carvings on local marble, engraved with astonishing skill and intricate detail and used to line the walls of the palace and its loggias with their large continuous surfaces. He also immortalized his deeds with huge statues. His son followed in his footsteps so that Nimrud came to be full of unique artistic works portraying the life of that period, including ivory artifacts of splendid artistry, of which Max Mallowan discovered many in a deep well in a corner of one of the palace's courtyards, apparently thrown in to be preserved from the hands of the Medians when they attacked the city.

The marble stela discovered that morning was not big but was in excellent condition, in addition to the fact that it was intricate and beautiful sculpture. The soil was still hanging on its edges, and I had hardly stretched out my hand to touch it when Hamilton prevented me, shouting, "No, no, please! It must be treated scientifically before anyone touches it . . ."

I jokingly asked him about its worth, and he replied, "It can't be valued at any price . . . One million dinars, at least. Most probably, it will be part of Iraq's share and go to the Iraqi Museum in Baghdad."

In the meantime, Max Mallowan had joined us, as joyful and excited as his colleague, and said, "You are the first two laypersons to see this wondrous find . . . Now, please come with us, for Mrs. Mallowan is expecting you."

In the shade of a long metal roof, we saw Agatha Christie with her secretary and two or three archaeologists, including

Professor Weismann, the cuneiform expert who had deciphered the writing engraved on Shalmaneser's stela. We found out that he could read cuneiform engravings as easily as one would read Arabic or English. The great novelist had prepared an English tea for us, with some cold milk, pastries, butter, and jam, like any lady at home in London. We joined them all in celebrating one more important discovery that added a new detail to our knowledge of the great history of Mesopotamia.

On that day, I saw the small room built of sun-baked mud bricks, which Agatha Christie had made into her study, tucked away amid the ruins, the statues of winged oxen, and the carved marble murals that were part of the royal palace and within sight of a huge marble head lying on the ground, which Mallowan said was the first statue Layard had discovered there in 1845, and he added that the workers excavating it from the earth began to jump and shout, exclaiming they had discovered the head of Nimrud the Giant.

When in the summer of 1986 I visited Nimrud for the third or fourth time—thirty-five years after this first visit—it was in the sweltering heat of August's sun and in the company of the members of the Association of Art Critics of Iraq. My colleagues and I experienced the same old ecstasy at seeing the remains of those ever-amazing sculptures. We then visited a closed room, the crude wooden door of which was unlocked for us by one of the site's guards, and lo and behold, it was Agatha Christie's same little room. It was preserved as it had been in the 1940s and the 1950s, and despite its very small size, she had made it into an English room, including an English fireplace and its traditional mantelpiece. In the fireplace, she used to burn logs of wood on cold nights, and by the light of an oil lamp, she would turn those implicit and explicit relationships and interconnected events that she had invented into "crimes," whose complicated plots she gave a magic that transcended time and place.

Most probably it was in the spring of that particular year (1951) in that little room of mud bricks, that she wrote her play entitled *The Mousetrap,* which was performed one year later in London and which had a phenomenal success and continued to be performed every night for thirty-five years, breaking all world records for continuous performance.

■　■　■

At the beginning of the 1960s, when Agatha Christie was over seventy years old and visited Baghdad less frequently than she did before, I asked her one day, "How many novels have you written so far?"

She said, "I counted them recently and found they were fifty-six novels. However, a few days ago I read an article about me in which the writer said I wrote sixty-two . . . I think that the writer of the article is nearer to the truth than I am." Then she added, laughing, "In fact, when the number is over fifty, the figure no longer has any importance."

I said, "Madam, the important thing is that one should always have something new to say that deserves being said."

At that remark, she asked me with gentle cunning, "And you, how many books have you written so far?"

I shook my head laughing, and I did not answer.

In fact, by that date I had published eight books, some I had authored and others I had translated. But when one is speaking with a writer who stopped counting her books after fifty, it's probably a virtue to remain silent about one's own small achievements.

 5

Princesses' Street

Every civilization in history has doubtlessly possessed people known as peripatetics, people who love to walk as simultaneous physical and mental exercise—the physical being a means to stimulate the mental—and whose thoughts were stirred as they walked two by two or in larger numbers. They might confine their walks to a limited, enclosed area, like a park or a garden, which they would traverse back and forth in search of more matters to discuss regarding the mind, emotions, and human behavior, thus arriving by their peripatetic discussions at what they might not have been able to, had they remained seated in their rooms.

It might be the custom of some of these peripatetics to walk by themselves, thoughts coming to each with the rhythm of his walking so that memories flock to him and ideas hasten, sometimes strange and sometimes bold, amazing, revealing, or disturbing; but the thoughts come as mere associations like daydreams that then vanish as soon as the person stops walking.

We know that many ideas crystallized in the minds of Greek philosophers as they walked for long hours in Plato's Academy and in Aristotle's, and there is no doubt that Socrates, the father of them all, was one of the greatest peripatetics.

It gives me great pleasure to say that, since my early life, I have been a peripatetic. In my childhood, and in my boyhood up to the age of fifteen, I rode in a carriage or a car only a few times. I walked from home to school and back, accompanied by friends who, like me, never stopped talking and wrangling. We reached our homes always refreshed (I never say tired), and we had a huge appetite for whatever food was available and for more talking and wrangling, and for more walking in any direction.

If it was often said that the roads we walked on and filled with talk of every kind had mercilessly worn out our shoes, we used to say that we were the ones who wore out the roads with our shoes, even with our bare feet at one time, ceaselessly walking up and down and in every direction.

Growing up with this peripatetic exercise helped me a lot when I was admitted to the Arab College in the fall of 1935, after it had moved to its new buildings on Mount al-Mukabbir in the southern suburbs of Jerusalem at a not inconsiderable distance from the main road to Bethlehem. When I took the bus from the station, which was quite a distance from our home in Jawrat al-Unnab, I got off at a crossroad and walked about two kilometers to reach the college. I had to traverse the same distance at noon to go to a shop where I had lunch; then I returned to college. In the evening, I again walked to the bus. I often missed the bus and walked all the way home, carrying my books and copybooks.

In the spring of 1936, our studies in all the schools of Palestine were interrupted because of the famous general strike in which the Palestinians once again rebelled against the British Mandate. The strike lasted about eleven months, and not a single bus, carriage, or wheeled vehicle of any kind ran on the roads, not even bicycles. Walking was our only transportation, and we had to do it . . . As my elder brother Murad still lived in Bethlehem, on the upper floor of a house on al-Najma Street overlooking the hills and eastern valleys of Bethlehem, I often walked about ten kilometers from our home in Jerusalem to my brother's in Bethlehem, accompanied by my brother Yousuf or some friends, talking and talking on the way and looking at people, houses, rocks, plants, and flowers again and again on every trip. At my brother's home, I sometimes met a young girl from the neighborhood, toward whom my adolescent heart had become inclined.

On one of those trips, I went up onto the roof of my brother's home. On the cement lining of the broad stone wall surrounding the roof, I innocently drew a young man playing an accordion (as I did in those days) with a gypsy woman dancing in front of him as he sang words I wrote in English, "Songs, wine, and beautiful women are the sweetest things in life." It so happened that the first person to see the picture and read the words, for she had learned some English at one of the nuns' schools, was the landlord's daughter, who was not the girl I had in mind. She immediately went downstairs to my brother's wife and protested what she called "the love message" I had drawn on the wall!

By necessity or by choice, walking remained for many years a pleasure for me and some of my friends, and a source of our physical and intellectual vitality. Perhaps in the early days of our friendship in 1938 and 1939, Ali Kamal and I walked hundreds of miles whenever he came from Tulkarm or from Beirut, where he was a student at the American University while I was still in Jerusalem waiting to go to England for my advanced studies. Not for one minute did we stop discussing and debating as we walked, with Arabic and English books in our hands and in our pockets.

We exchanged thoughts that swirled in our heads and burst on our tongues, wonderful and bold thoughts about everything in the world that could be seen and that could not, and we promised ourselves that we would transform them all into writings as no writer ever had, works that would change life and thought, and allow human hands to reach the stars of heaven . . .

As years passed, my inclination to walk remained alive wherever I went. I am not an enthusiast of sports and athletic games. The only game I liked and played when I was a student at the Arab College was tennis. However, no sooner had I left college at the age of eighteen than I abandoned tennis too, although I had a good racket that I kept for many years later and that continued to entice me but that I did not use again, even in England, the country of sports lovers. Walking for me continued to substitute for all other sports perhaps because, since my boyhood, I found that it ceaselessly brought ideas to me. Through it, I would discover not only the beauties of nature and its little enjoyable details, especially if I walked in the fields (Ah for the charming fields and valleys of Jerusalem!), but also the relations between things, between abstract ideas, between my old experiences and the new ones I was going through daily. Between me and some of the places I walked at every stage of my life, there arose a love that is difficult to speak about fully, as is the case with every love.

When I was at the Home Hospitality Hotel in Stratford-upon-Avon, Shakespeare's birthplace, I remember once on a cold morning openly expressing my love for walking in the English countryside. I was talking to another guest who said he too loved walking, so we agreed to go out together after lunch. I was twenty years old, and he was forty-five or older. At the appointed time, I saw him coming downstairs from his room, having put on a thick overcoat and large boots and wrapped himself with a woolen scarf. He said, "Come on!" As for me, I had my ordinary shoes on, and I preferred to leave my overcoat in my room lest it should burden me. And we took off. We walked. We walked briskly and fast. My damned English friend did not slow down, nor did he stop talking. Even though I was the lover of walking that I was, I waited for the word saying it was time to return, but the matter was not of concern to him. I looked at my watch and desperately said, "Ho! Two hours and a half have passed!" He answered, "The day has still more hours." He continued to walk, so I had to offer some pretext and say I had an appointment at the hotel. So he agreed to stop, hit his chest with his fists, took a deep breath, and said, "I feel great! How about you?" I said, "Me too!" We turned around and walked back for more than two hours. I reached the hotel exhausted, hungry, and thirsty—for that was the longest walk I had ever taken, a fast one and without a break. I still remember how good the tea was that I drank and how delicious the supper that I devoured that evening.

■　■　■

During the preceding quarter of a century, the mature period of my life, and after my love for a number of places where I walked had arisen, there arose in me a deep affection for Princesses' Street in the al-Mansour neighborhood of Baghdad, and I still enjoy its pulse and the emotions it evokes.

It was easy for me to get acquainted with this street, distinguished as it was among all the streets of Baghdad; for it was near and parallel to the street on which I had chosen in 1956 to buy a plot of land within a residential development area, paid for in installments, the last of which I paid twenty-one years later. On this land, I intended to build a house that would satisfy my family's needs at that time. Professor Ali Haydar al-Rikabi, an intimate friend of mine, was the president of the al-Mansour Land Company, and he advised me to buy that lot, which at that time was no more than a small rectangle on a large map. It had originally been part of a spacious garden that had been transformed into a modern, well-planned residential area at one end of which had been established the new race track, to which horse racing gradually moved from New Baghdad. On this land also the al-Mansour Club was established in those days, and it officially opened in the early 1950s under the presidency of Ali Haydar al-Rikabi also, and I was one of its first members.

For purely financial reasons, I could not finish building my home until six years later, although I was perhaps the first to buy a lot on that street at a time when it was paved in a primitive way, had many poor people's shacks on it, and had cows and sheep grazing freely on it. Gradually within a short period of time, houses were built on both sides at far distances from one another, and palm trees in two long, parallel lines were planted and soon became fully grown along the edges of its broad sidewalks. When we finally moved to our home in September of 1962, the street had begun to acquire a distinct character, especially as I preferred in those days to beautify the sidewalk along the front of my house by planting grass, roses, and pine trees in it. The neighbors soon tore out their concrete sidewalks and planted grass and roses. That was the beginning of the pattern that was followed by everyone who later built a home in the al-Mansour neighborhood— making the sidewalk a continuous part of his front garden with grass and annual and perennial flowers.

It pleases me to mention that the first person to draw a plan for my house was my old friend, the architect Qahtan Awni, our intimate relationship going back to the early 1950s before either of us was married. We both participated in establishing the Baghdad Modern Art Group with Jawad Salim in the spring of 1951. But his plan of my house remained unimplemented because I was late to begin the actual building. My friend, the architect Rifat al-Jadirji, offered another plan in 1961, and it utterly differed from Qahtan Awni's. So in the end, I decided to benefit from both plans and designed a third of my own. (And how my architect friends reproached me for my brazenness!) It was closer to what I myself wanted, namely a home for me, my wife, and my two little sons, a home that was within my financial means, which were unfortunately limited. I made the plan wholly dependent on a principle of straight crossing lines, without exaggerating the size of the windows. Qahtan Awni had been especially inclined to make the windows almost as large in height and width as the walls of every room, as though we were living in Berkeley, California, where he had studied architecture. It so happened that I went as a visiting professor to this university in the company of my wife fourteen years later.

As soon as I was settled in our new home, I resumed my pastime of walking, and I discovered that our nearness to Princesses' Street had made people call our street by that name too. That was not correct, of course, except that the people of Baghdad were accustomed to giving a name they liked to a certain street and soon afterward also giving it to nearby streets. A few years earlier, for example, we used to live in al-Azamiyya on a street called Taha Street, near the Farouq Mosque and the police station; I learned in those days that the real Taha Street was actually at some distance from our street and was named after Lieutenant General Taha al-Hashimi who had lived on it for many years; then the name "spread" to a number of nearby streets, including ours. It is worth mentioning that the official name of Taha Street according to the municipal sign hanging at its beginning is al-Khansa Street, but the popular usage has clung to it more strongly than its official name up to this day.

Princesses' Street itself acquired its name informally, for it was named by the people for the two Hashemite princesses who were among the first to build residences on it. One of them was Princess Badia, daughter of King Ali and younger sister of Prince Abd al-Ilah who was originally involved in transforming the spacious garden in the Dawoudi area into the neighborhood that was later named al-Mansour. The other princess was Princess Jalila, also daughter of King Ali and wife of Sharif Hazim. The two residences are still standing, with their distinctive yellowish color. After the Revolution of July 14, 1958, a famous sheep merchant bought the larger of the two and preserved the beauty of its entrance and front. The smaller, directly next door, had a number of owners, eventually becoming a public auction center well known to this day.

I think that naming this street was very appropriate, for it was named after the first and the most famous of those who resided on it. (This is a principle followed by many cities in other countries when naming their new streets.) The name is suitable for one of the most beautiful and impressive streets in Baghdad; it is distinguished by its west side adjoining an expanse of open land on which the race track and its annexes were established; it is also distinguished by the elegant residences on its east side and the southern part of its west side. Palm trees shade part of its southern extension, but most of its sidewalks are shaded by leafy eucalyptus trees, which in time have grown tall and continue to give the street its well-deserved dignity and freshness with their green color in all seasons. Furthermore, the street enjoys a quietness which is akin to that of the countryside because public buses hardly enter it, and so its air is sweet and tender because of the green fields of the race track. All this and its beautiful straight perspective through the trees make promenading on it enticing. The street is not much more than one kilometer in length and has two lanes separated by islands in which sway the perennials that explode with red and violet on most days of the year. It is known that an Indian gardening architect, who used to work at al-Habbiniyya in the 1940s, participated in planning the gardens of this area and imported from India the eucalyptus trees known for their repelling mosquitoes as well as other kinds of decorative tropical trees that have later become a noticeable part of the city parks. This continued the tradition of importing seedlings and plants from India begun in the 1920s.

I remembered Princesses' Street with great pride when I visited India and Pakistan in 1988 and observed that many modern streets in New Delhi and Islamabad were shady because the branches of the tall trees growing on opposite sides of the street met in an open arch in the sky, giving the impression as one drove one's car through it, that one was going through a street winding in a vast public park.

Since we are talking about parks, we should mention that on the southern part of Princesses' Street there is a large park of dense green that on its broad side is connected with our street. The park has two gates, one on our street and the other on Princesses' Street. Despite recent neglect, the park continues to attract soccer-loving boys who on certain afternoons play in one of its open squares enclosed by roses of various kinds; and young groups set up a camp in the open from season to season, and the park is then astir with their movement and shouts.

I mention this park because, when we first moved to our

house, I often took my two small sons to play in it. I also took them to Princesses' Street on days when there was horse racing; I used to carry each on my shoulder so that they could see the elegance of the horses over the iron fence. Spectators standing on the sidewalk outside the fence had their own way of betting on the horses without entering the racetrack. We all enjoyed the horses and the sound of their hooves as they broke from the starting line, for they raised a cloud of dust and swam in it as they went around the track. Those who crowded the bleachers on the other side of the fence and who had bet on the horses got excited, and their shouts reached a thrilling climax and then quickly subsided, simultaneously conveying the sorrow of the losers and the ecstasy of the winners.

Then there came a time, in the middle of the 1980s when I began to take my granddaughter Dima walking with me on Princesses' Street and raised her on my shoulder to look at the horses as I had her father earlier. When she was ten years old, she began to accompany me on my walks almost every afternoon on her bicycle. I walked, and she rode her bicycle ahead of me a little, then returned to accompany me for some distance and went again ahead of me a little, and so on, until we returned home together, each in his or her way.

This was our custom for most of the days of the "thirty-day aggression,"* during which God wished to grant us amazing sunny weather that enticed us to go out in the open air. Many of the inhabitants of the neighborhood had deserted their houses and gone to remote and more secure villages, but I remained with my family at our house. I often went out for a walk after three o'clock in the afternoon when glass strewn from the windows broken in the nighttime air raids sparkled all along the sidewalks. I found out that if I went to the right and walked to the end of our street and then entered al-Mansour Street, everything was fine there. Once when I turned to the left and walked along the park's edge and entered Princesses' Street, the air-raid warning siren went off. But I continued to walk in the wonderful bright sun alone,

---

*The massive aerial bombardment of Baghdad, starting from January 16–17, 1991, during Operation Desert Storm in the Gulf War. (Translator's note.)

under the blue sky in which I sometimes saw the enemy airplanes soaring like loathsome flies going to their murderous goals.

I will never forget when, wrapped as usual in my peripatetic thoughts, I was walking during one of the daytime air raids and was suddenly faced with a rose bush on a sidewalk near our house. It had a large red rose on an elegant stem leaning toward me. It swayed, proud of itself, and made me stop to admire it: splendid, bold, pulsating with vitality, asking me to express delight and love that was its right. Here was blooming life, with a promise of a greater bloom and richer life; and above us were the damned flies coming from the regions of hatred and death, buzzing with omens of murder and ferocity, and demanding our blood . . .

Naturally, I was not the only one to be fascinated with the beauty of Princesses' Street and our own street parallel to it. There were many people who had the financial means to buy large plots of land—from 1600 to more than 3000 square meters each— on these streets and the side streets branching off them, and they built remarkable residences with eye-catching architecture and gardens. After we moved to our house, it pleased me that a number of my close friends made efforts to obtain lots near us or on the side streets that flourished. By the beginning of the 1970s, they had established themselves in their new homes, each a few minutes' walk from ours. Now and then, we went out together for relaxed and slow walks, for I don't like quick pace in this pursuit of mine. I prefer a leisurely walk because walking briskly as athletes do is a sport in itself. I, on the other hand, want exercise of thought, discussion, and creation of ideas from walking in addition to physical exercise, and this does not happen unless we walk slowly and purposefully.

There were others whom we did not know and who discovered the joy of walking in this neighborhood of ours that combined beauty, quiet, and little traffic. Toward the end of the 1960s and especially during the 1970s, I noticed that couples came frequently to our street, particularly in the long afternoons. They seemed to be "strangers" who had come from far neighborhoods, having found in our street a place where they could be alone with each other in their promenade, where no one knew them and where they dared walk hand in hand or arm in arm. Unawares, we started hearing that our street came to be called Lovers' Street. They sometimes came in their cars, got out, and walked together on the street or went to the park and lost themselves in its rosy labyrinths. It seems that as soon as these lovers got married, it did not occur to them to continue their walks in our neighborhood, thank God. Most probably, they never went for a walk at all after they got married. And thus, our neighborhood remained very quiet and had little activity, and its lovers changed but they did not grow in numbers.

In point of fact, those who walked with their wives on Princesses' Street or our street were very rare. Most were foreigners, and we recognized them as such by their blond hair and blue eyes and the tracksuits most preferred to wear when running. Our own wives, however much they loved nature, rarely thought of walking in the manner of peripatetics, even if they sometimes wore tracksuits while doing household chores. My dear wife is not an exception and, like all my friends' wives, washed her hands of long walks. It was as if she freed me each time I went out to be alone in my own manner; then I would return to her with a new idea that had begun to take shape in my head.

As years passed by, innumerable ideas crystallized in my mind and were accompanied by fantasies and images, and even by expressions with which I tried to capture all or some of them as I walked in the shade of the eucalyptus trees on Princesses' Street or in the shade of the palm trees of its twin. Never was I heedless of the fact that each of the two sides of the street had a long line of palms, not only to emphasize its straightness, but—I dare say—its tenderness, as the dense palm leaves bent downward with the elegance of parasols to shed their continuous shade on the street and the sidewalks. In summer, their green tops glowed with clusters of dates, green at first, then yellow like golden bunches dangling their bounty, then changing at summer's end to that alluring brown that announced that the dates had ripened and it was time to pick them. But there was no one to pick them, for the residents did not regard them as dates to be eaten, perhaps because they were not of the *barhi,* or the *barban,* or the *ashrasi,* or the *maktoum,* or the *surrat al-khatoun* variety but of the *zahdi*, more abundant in Iraq than any other—even though its fruit is big and beautiful and, when ripe, has the taste of English toffee. The dates fell abundantly on the sidewalks and when October arrived, passers-by walked on sidewalks copiously strewn with dates from the beginning to the end of the street and its side streets. And let him who wants them pick them!

Although only a few of the neighborhood's residents cared to pollinate the palms shading their homes, nature had its own clever tricks of pollination and multiplication. In summer, clusters of dates once more dangled from the palm trees, green, then golden yellow, and they later strewed the sidewalks with their date generosity again.

At the beginning of the 1980s, when I began to work with a group of dear friends as editor of a magazine called *Funoun Arabiyya* (Arab Arts), I frequented Princesses' Street increasingly, either on foot or in my car, because the editorial office of the magazine was on a nearby street. In those days, my writings followed one after the other, both short and long, and it was perhaps on those trips back and forth that I subjected them to scrutiny; many of them later appeared in my books: *al-Fann wa-l-Hulm, wa-l-Fil* (Art, Dreams, and Action), *Ta'ammulat fi Bunyan Marmari* (Meditations on a Marble Structure), and *Muayashat al-Namira* (Living with the Tigress).

The birth, the growth, and the completion of my novel, *al-Ghuraf al-Ukhra* (The Other Rooms), occurred on Princesses' Street; likewise, the chapters of my autobiography, *al-Bi'r al-Oula* (The First Well), which carried me to the days and places of my childhood as though in the arms of a genie from *Alf Layla wa Layla* (One Thousand and One Nights), who was accustomed to making his way through to distant lands and past times. Whenever I returned home from Princesses' Street to write, I was like one returning from the valleys of Bethlehem and the hills of Jerusalem; for I was filled with the fragrance and visions of those valleys and hills, and with the fragrance and visions of the eucalyptus and palm trees and the flowers on our street. My latest novel, *Yawmiyyat Sarab Affan* (Diaries of Sarab Affan), was not only inspired by the sweet aromas of this street, but it also conveyed many of its details and colors, its rain and sunshine. As for my novel, *al-Bahth an Walid Masoud* (Search for Walid Masoud), it contains complete pages that took form and content as I was rapturously drifting on our two streets.

This is of no less importance than what, since the end of the 1950s, the news conveyed about the lives of some of the residents of this neighborhood, with its two parallel streets. Some of the news items were pleasing (and they were many); and some were disturbingly tragic, and these had perhaps a deeper and greater effect on one's soul. There were those who were martyred in the war, those whose married lives were wrecked, those who emigrated in despair, those who went mad, those who were killed, and those who committed suicide. To see such events happen to people who were your neighbors and visited you, whom you knew and visited, and to people whom you loved and who loved you reminds you constantly that this small neighborhood that you reside in is nothing but one small part of the larger society. It may appear quiet on the surface but, deep down, it boils like a kettle, human emotions like volcanoes in the depths of the ocean, not visible to the eye but erupting from time to time and causing tidal waves in which many are drowned. Every walk on a sunny or a cloudy day is a contemplation on this smaller world that contains the larger world condensed in its heart, with all its vicissitudes, its ecstasies, its madnesses. What you find is that some residents change and some houses are sold to new buyers and are then pulled down to be rebuilt in accordance with the tastes of the nouveaux riches, but the turbulent depths remain the same.

With all that I have seen in my life over the years, all the pleasures and pains, all the joys and sorrows, all the love and anguish that weave an old/new canvas for me on their loom, I continue to seek intellectual exercise and recreative diversion in my walks. Perhaps with time, I walk slower than I did in the past; but I am still peripatetic and will be so long as the muscles in my legs don't fully fail me.

Here, I have to inject a small note, which I would not have made to those in authority, if it were not for this old abiding love of mine. Why in heaven's name have the sidewalks of all the streets in the neighborhood been paved with a fine surface that is easy to walk on, and yet when Princesses' Street's turn came in the middle 1980s, the road itself was paved with the best technology so as to be of the highest efficiency for cars to drive on, but its sidewalks were harshly and haphazardly paved with the least possible care? A mixture of asphalt and gravel was simply thrown on the ground—and what gravel! The sidewalks are merely random and unconnected patches of lumps, protrusions, and unevenness, the likes of which are only seen in rugged mountain paths, and it is difficult to walk on them. In order to avoid being hurt, we pedestrians have to get off the sidewalk and down onto the edge of the smooth and comfortable road and share it with the cars, all the while taking care of any unexpected hazards.

In addition to all this, these wide sidewalks have in time accumulated piles of dry leaves, branches, and bark that has fallen from the eucalyptus trees, along with shards of glass, empty cans, and waste of all kinds left by those who bet on horses in the three afternoons of racing each week. It seems that nobody will ever be concerned, unless a stormy wind one day throws down a big worm-eaten old tree and the way is blocked completely. Don't peripatetics and pedestrians, including students of a large nearby school, have a right to walk comfortably on their feet, as cars and buses have a right to roll comfortably on their wheels?

■　■　■

At one time I used to wonder when I finished a new book: "How many cups of coffee have I drunk to write this book? And how many pipes have I smoked? And how many records and tapes have I listened to?"

In recent years, I realized that I also had to wonder: "And how many kilometers in how many walks and outings have I walked on Princesses' Street to write what I have written?"

6

(in twelve sections)

Lamiᶜa and the Annus Mirabilis

I try, I try every day
To regain you from the kingdom of the invisible,
Vivacious and laughing as
You always were vivacious and laughing
In the days when you were crazy, along with me,
As though life, despite its tragedies, remained
A huge joke that did not deserve anything
From us but laughter after weeping.
With a magic touch of your hands
You make a jubilant garden
Out of seven roses;
And out of one home, our home,
You make a poem for the eyes,
Which is renewed every forenoon
With its rhythms and its meanings.
Return, then, to my hands as you
Sing and clap
And as you read poetry to me
While your sleeves expose
Your shoulders and display
A neck that I call
The most beautiful neck in Baghdad
On the most beautiful shoulders
That have ever been dreamt of
By a genius-sculptor in Babylon or Athens.

Lami^ca

Line drawing in ink by Jabra (1952)

(1)

The academic year 1949–50 was the second year after my arrival in Baghdad to work as a professor of English literature at the College of Arts and Sciences, established that year. That year witnessed my broad openness to Baghdad, and Baghdad's openness to me in a way I had never expected or dreamt of. I began to make the acquaintance of many people, both men and women, from all walks of cultural and social life as I had in the previous year, but the circles began to expand and the paths to branch in every direction.

I was kept in a state of constant activity, divided between my teaching duties and the joy of meeting people. In addition, I wrote, painted, gave public lectures in various places, and sometimes translated, especially for the journal of the Iraqi Academy.

The Department of English Literature in the College of Arts, where I taught, was a department I had established in the fall of 1949 with my colleague Desmond Stewart under the supervision of Dr. Abd al-Aziz al-Douri, the dean at that time. I also lectured at the Higher Teachers' College during the time Dr. Abd al-Hamid Kazim was dean, as well as at Queen Aliya College for Girls during the deanship of Mrs. Amat al-Said. The buildings of the last were across the street from the College of Arts. As for the Higher Teachers' College, it was at some distance, and so whenever I finished lecturing at Arts or Queen Aliya, I took a two-horse carriage from among the many that still filled Baghdad's streets and roads, and I relaxed on its old leather seat as the horse ambled to Teachers' College at a stimulating rhythm that brought me there in less than ten minutes. The coachman charged me no more than fifty fils (that is, one dirham—the dinar having twenty dirhams). He often suggested that he wait for me until I finished giving my lecture, in order to take me back to my base at Arts, at a charge of one more dirham.

At all these colleges, I participated in the activities of the students. Extracurricular societies were established for them: there was a debating society, using Arabic and sometimes English; another society for drama; and a third for music. We often had guests attending these activities, intellectuals from the city, as well as students and professors from other colleges. In those days, I supervised a new studio at the College of Arts for those students who loved painting, and I also used to paint with them, until Professor Hafiz al-Duroubi took it over from me upon his return from England, where he had studied art. (From these amateurs, he formed the Impressionists Group two or three years later, which included some who had begun with me at the studio and who would later become famous artists: Muzaffar al-Nawwab, Hayat Jamil Hafiz, and Abd al-Amir al-Qazzaz. They were joined by other artists, some of whom were amateurs as well and who also became famous, such as Dr. Ala Bashir and Yasin Shakir.)

Meanwhile, I continued to write short stories, essays, and poems, and I published them in *al-Adib,* a Beirut monthly magazine owned by Albert Adib, which at that time was the cause of much interest and excitement because it attracted the young and the innovative in the Arab world. I don't know how I had time that year to also give private lessons to some young men and women in my room at the Baghdad Hotel. This was a tenth-grade hotel on al-Rashid Street, on the edge of the Murabbaa Neighborhood, near the popular al-Zawra Cinema. The noise of the dialogue and music of the movies in this cinema shown at the lowest prices used to reach me during the night.

My little room overlooking the inner courtyard of the hotel was hardly large enough for a narrow bed, an old sofa, a straight-backed chair, a table for writing (which I had myself bought for two dinars when I began working a year earlier), and a movable Aladdin heater that I also used to make tea and coffee in a large kettle. I decorated the walls with oil paintings that I had done in Jerusalem and Bethlehem and with some new paintings that were beginning to increase in number. That year, this room was the meeting place of many of the most well-known of Iraq's writers, artists, and professors whose ages ranged from twenty-two to thirty-two, and it daily witnessed animated discussions about what was being written and painted in Baghdad and in all the other Arab capitals—as far as their news reached us.

Among those who came to my room were Buland al-Haydari, Adnan Raouf, Husayn Mirdan, Hilmi Samara, Jawad Salim, Desmond Stewart, Khalid al-Rahhal, Nizar Salim, Abd al-Malik Nouri, Najib al-Mani, Zuhdi Jarallah, Yousuf Abd al-Masih Tharwat, and many others. We were also within a stone's throw of the Swiss Café, which offered café au lait and *cassata* ice cream and was frequented by ladies of all ages, contrary to the custom of cafés in those days. Off to one side in the café was an electric gramophone with recordings of Bach, Brahms, and Tchaikovsky for those who liked to listen to them. Next to the Swiss Café was the famous Brazilian Café, which was more traditional than the Swiss Café and could hold many visitors, most of whom were intellectuals and journalists from the educated class of the city. This café was run by a highborn Syrian man, who liked to mix with his clientele and knew them by name and offered them the best Turkish coffee in town, which was made of Brazilian coffee beans, after which the coffee shop was named. He even had someone who would roast the coffee beans and grind them for those who desired to buy coffee to take out. Its intoxicating aroma filled the Murabbaa Neighborhood all along al-Rashid Street. (Perhaps he was the only one in Baghdad to sell fresh coffee until Captanian opened a shop nearby where I continued to buy ground coffee beans and tobacco for many years.)

Some of the writers were not happy at the Brazilian Café unless they sat on the front line chairs facing the street, which was always noisy and busy with its ever-changing scenes, people, colors, carriages, cars, and lottery ticket sellers shouting, "Five thousand dinars! Five thousand dinars!" The din did not cease until about midnight, especially because next to the café was a famous nightclub, in which Afifa Iskandar sang.*

Desmond Stewart introduced me to Afifa Iskandar at her request, for he used to give her private English lessons. To my surprise, I found her to be young, bright, and thirsty for knowledge

---

*Readers of my poem "Bayt min Hajar" (A Stone House) in my collection *Tammouz fi al-Madina* (Tammuz in the City) will find some of this atmosphere and some of the mood of those days, that I tried to suggest in this poem and in others of the same period.

and culture. Desmond and I used to boast that we were the only two men in Baghdad, on going to the nightclub, whom the "artiste" would offer a drink and pay for it, not the contrary.

At the beginning of June of 1950, that is, at the end of the academic year, I prepared to leave Baghdad carrying two paper bags that my friends had given me full of little, green, Iraqi apples notable for the Babylonian acidity that I liked. I intended to spend the summer at our home in Bethlehem on the West Bank, which had become part of the Hashemite Kingdom of Jordan at the time. Before I left, the College of Arts and Sciences had renewed my contract for a third year and given me a generous raise and paid me a lump sum in advance covering my salary for the summer months. I was then sure that my financial situation had sufficiently improved to allow me to rent a big room at a short distance from my old hotel. It was a room with a special balcony on the street and was in an elegant and very clean pension owned by a Greek lady named Athena, who was very gentle and very conservative. The pension was on the upper floor of a new building, next to the Tigris Palace, one of the well-known hotels of Baghdad, and a few steps' distant from the two biggest and most important hotels in Baghdad at that time, namely the Semiramis and the Sindbad hotels overlooking the Tigris. There, I used to take most of my lunches and dinners, and entertain my friends whenever an occasion arose, especially the Sindbad.

However, the most important thing to happen in that year, after I returned from Bethlehem at the beginning of October to resume teaching, was that its activities and the men and women I met in it set in motion the events of the following year, 1951. It was an amazing year that witnessed great social effervescence, intellectual opulence, and emotional generosity. It was a year in my life that can be rightly called annus mirabilis, and in it I turned thirty-one.

But here, I will focus on one main thread of events among many that interwove to form the texture of that year, each of which, if one had unending time, deserves to be specially followed up in detail in order to bring out the beauty and complexity of the whole. The main thread was my meeting the most wonderful woman in my life, the one who gave everything that happened to both of us at the time and in later years a magic in which all the meanings of life converged. This was true not only as far as the persons and relationships that enriched one another and the continuous experiences with all their pleasures, torments, and contradictions, but also as far as the creative acts that gave experience itself deep value and permanent uniqueness.

■ ■ ■

To A——

You listen to my words as I utter them
In a foreign tongue, and you try
To understand their meanings, your charmed eyes
Growing larger and shining at every gesture of mine;
And I know that you listen and are preoccupied
With my description of "shivering tones"
And "the soul with all its anguish"
And "the blue of distant horizons"—inducing you
Sometimes to smile a tender smile,
A pure smile that arises from
The crystalline beauty of your
Eighteen years of age.
How often have I wished that it was you
Who spoke and I who listened,
Despite my knowledge that every motion
Of your lips and of your locks of hair
Pushed back with your lily-white hand,
Will cloud my understanding. At that moment,
I will understand only with my eyes,
And I will try with every look of mine
To solve another one
Of the problems of beauty
That never end.

With these words toward the end of 1949, I described in English the beauty of one of my female students, and I don't remember whether I gave her the poem. Most probably, I wised up and was prudent and let her know about it only indirectly, as when I would read the poem to a group of students that included her. For Arabs, flirting in verse (even if it is in English), is forgivable; I often saw turbaned old men who would do it with pleasure in front of others, hoping that some of their words would reach the beautiful woman for whom it was intended.

A few days before writing this poem, I had written another, but with exactly opposite sentiments; it was very bitter and in it I complained of

> These surging faces, these eyes which
> Are countless, belong to men, men, men
> Wherever I turn: Oh, how horrible!

And I complained of the bragging of men that I heard and the ugliness that assailed me; I complained of the ringing words that always echoed and that I always met with silence, a silence that I learned to fill myself with, "a silence as deep as the running waters of the Tigris."

I had to seek beauty, for it had been my usual companion in previous years. But I found that I had almost forgotten it for about two years, when I was in exile and suffering the ordeal of the diaspora.

There is no doubt that during the following year I enjoyed an incandescence of some kind because of the feeling that I was finally surrounded by youthful beauty that appeared to me in a kind of twilight state between illusion and reality. I touched it, and I touched it not. Yet it allowed me to experience a sensual, defiant rebelliousness afire with youth and freshness—that defiant rebelliousness in which I did not know whether I was the one who chased or the one who was chased.

■ ■ ■

She laughed and laughed as though she knew that there was some irresistible magic in her laugh. She held a tennis racket under her arm and was wearing a short, white skirt that showed the beauty of her legs and knees. She wore a white blouse with an open neck and short sleeves and had on tennis shoes. In her hand, she had a small paper bag full of jujubes, which have a yellowish orange color when ripe and are very sweet in the spring. It was the last day of March 1951. Will I ever forget this date that decided the direction of my life? She filled my eyes as though all the women and goddesses of the Italian Renaissance paintings, all the women of all the world's painters, the women with locks flying in the air, the women playing among the branches and running around the rose bushes were finally embodied in one woman—a woman with large black eyes and two locks of her short hair hanging playfully on her forehead, a woman whose lips were sculpted of coral, whose teeth endowed her smile with the brilliance of pearls about which a thousand Arab poets have sung. She filled my eyes, she filled my heart, she filled all my being with a seductive charm I was not ready for. She took one jujube at a time from the paper bag, tossed it up in the air, then opened her mouth and caught it between her laughing teeth as it fell. I observed her in amazement, while she continued to toss the jujubes high up in the air and to catch them between her beautiful teeth.

"Lamiᶜa! Lamiᶜa!" shouted Sahira. "Be serious, at least for one moment . . . Let me introduce you to . . ."

Lamiᶜa stopped playing with the jujubes to say, "I know, I know . . . the professor . . . I see him every day at Teachers' College, surrounded by male and female students, especially female students . . . We're honored, Professor . . . Hello Adnan. Where is Nihad?"

It soon became clear that my friend Adnan Raouf had been a classmate of Lamiᶜa's brother Amer at the College of Law, where they had graduated at the same time, and I learned that he was a friend of the family's since those days. As for Nihad, she was a beautiful Christian young woman and had been a close friend of Lamiᶜa since the time they were both students at university, and Adnan's story with her was famous in those days for its sorrow.

With speed, with strange speed, our group came together: Adnan and I, and three or four other friends, one of whom was also called Adnan and had recently established a legal practice, and another was Mahmoud al-Hout, the Palestinian poet who was my colleague at the College of Arts and Sciences. The center of our attention was Lamiᶜa and Sahira, and we addressed our words and comments to them, and they responded fluently and in a charming, winsome manner. Both had master's degrees in English literature and were teaching it at the university level. Adnan Ra'ouf enjoyed showing off his competence in English, which he had learned with all its minutiae by his own effort. We therefore conversed in English, exchanging jokes and common expressions—which doubtlessly annoyed our other friends.

We did not hesitate and suggested in a low voice and in English that Adnan Ra'ouf and I, along with Lamiᶜa and Sahira, should go to the Sindbad Hotel for dinner—without the others, of course. We outwitted the others with what we thought to be the cunning of conspirators, and we left with the two young ladies. We first went to Lamiᶜa's home, which was a five-minute walk from Antar Square (where the Olympic Club had been recently built); there she changed her clothes, and then we all took a taxi to al-Rashid Street.

Hardly had we entered the Sindbad Hotel and sat down in the dining room when we saw two of the friends we had left behind at the club entering and going to the bar. They sat near the entrance and observed us, seething with indignation. But who of us would let such a matter bother him at a moment like that, after having been able to be alone at the dining table with those we liked. It was a great dinner: the first of many dinners and lunches that Lamiᶜa and I would have together at this restaurant, served by the same two waiters, Ilyas and Hanna, for many months, rather years, afterwards.

Sahira had just returned from America a few weeks earlier and was a professor of English literature at Queen Aliya College, where I worked with her. I myself had just returned from an exciting trip to the north of Iraq where in the company of Zayd Ahmad Uthman I had visited for the first time a number of the area's towns, villages, and archaeological landmarks including Irbil, Mosul, Nineveh, Nimrud, which had been the capital of the ancient Assyrians, and had seen its amazing digs in the company of Agatha Christie and her husband Max Mallowan. I was ready for further sightseeing and exploration and for further immersion in the joys of the eyes and the intellect. When Sahira learned that I also lectured at the Higher Teachers' College (in addition to my work at the College of Arts and Sciences), she asked me, "Have you met my friend Lami^{c}a al-Askari at the Higher Teachers' College?" When I answered, "I don't think so," she said, "It's impossible that she would escape your attention . . . A dark-skinned young woman with big eyes, who had returned from university a few months before I did and was appointed to a position there."

I asked out of the blue, "Do you mean that dark-skinned professor with a glum face who does not smile to anyone or anything, even a hot, freshly baked loaf of bread?"

Sahira laughed, amazed, and said, "Glum face? Does not smile? She is the merriest young woman I have ever known!"

I then remembered that this young professor was, one day, sitting near me in the staff room of the English Department at Teachers' College during the break between lectures. I was talking to the chairman of the department, Professor Zebedee, about a famous American short-story writer named Damon Runyon, who had died recently, and about his book *Guys and Dolls*.

I turned to the lady sitting at my right and quite innocently asked her in English what she thought of him in order to let her participate in the conversation. She surprisingly frowned more severely and answered without looking at me, "I know nothing about him." Her tone gave the impression that she was saying, "Don't you be so clever with me, man!" And she got up and left us.

I related this event to Sahira, and she laughed again and said, "It's acting, Professor, just acting! Lami^{c}a is my friend from school days, and we went together to America for our university education—but she returned before I did because she is more intelligent than I am."

I noted that Sahira was blond and had blue eyes, whereas her friend was dark-skinned and had black eyes. It seems she felt what I was thinking and said, "We were always together and they called us 'Black and White,' (after a famous brand of whisky) . . . Listen, we'll surprise her tomorrow at the Olympic Club, for tomorrow is the day on which Lamiᶜa plays tennis there. Will you come with me? You'll see many of your friends there too, no doubt . . ."

■ ■ ■

At the dinner table, I raised this subject, and Lamiᶜa said, "Well, most of the students I teach are young men, some of whom are almost my age, if not older. I therefore have to be very cautious; I'm still in my first year of teaching. Many of the assigned English texts are love poems and sonnets. That's why I have to be exceedingly serious and wear a mask of sullenness, even with professors . . . As for you, Professor, I see that whenever you finish lecturing, you dally with the students, you trifle and jest with them; and wherever you go, the female students besiege you insistently, and you seem to enjoy that . . . When I saw you so besieged for the first time, I said to myself, 'I must avoid this man lest he should imagine that I am competing with those silly girls for his attention.'"

And this was exactly what she had done since that day and caused me to fall into a beautiful tribulation. The young woman who had dominated my attention for two or three months until I came to know Lamiᶜa was a twenty-year-old student. She was the most intelligent and most prominent student in the class I taught English poetry and translation to. She was distinguished from all her classmates by her beauty and strong personality. She was conservative and came from a highborn family; every morning, a chauffeur brought her to college in a magnificent car that returned to take her home at the end of the day, so that she would not have to ride public buses and mix with common people. Her aristocratic bearing was one of the reasons I was fascinated by her. She reminded me of the poet I loved in my early youth, whose life and poetry had a permanent influence on me, namely, the English poet Percy Bysshe Shelley. He was married to Mary Godwin and became attached to an aristocratic

Italian young woman in Genoa who gave him the impression she was a prisoner of her family. He imagined that he wanted to save her and free her from her prison . . . Italy at the beginning of the nineteenth century, and Baghdad in the middle of the twentieth: here they met in this very clandestine relationship that excited both of us.

All of a sudden I found myself pulled in opposite directions: my student and Lamiᶜa. As for Lamiᶜa, with a master's degree from the University of Wisconsin at Madison, she was rightly a lady in full control of herself; at twenty-five years old, she knew exactly what she wanted and in what direction she should move. Her freedom was her dearest treasure, and she had many quite distinguished male and female friends. Since the death of her father Muhammad Barqi al-Askari, a former brigadier general and later a member of parliament, she had become quite the apple of her mother's eye, despite the fact that she had an older brother, Amer, who had become governor of Zammar, a northern county in the district of Mosul. Lamiᶜa was also the niece of General Bakr Sidqi al-Askari, who was the first person in modern Arab history to stage a military coup d'état: in 1936 he rose in support of the man he loved and revered, King Ghazi, son of Faysal I, giving his life as a price less than a year after the coup when he was assassinated by the opposing factions. All this left an aura around Lamiᶜa, which gave the impression of remoteness from most people, perhaps even of superiority since the time she was a student at the Higher Teachers' College and attracted attention wherever she went. I shall never forget how one of my colleagues at the college, a graduate of the University of Oxford, was amazed when he learned that I had a friendly relationship with Lamiᶜa, I who was a stranger from Palestine and she who was famous for her beauty, dignity, and social background. He said, "Lamiᶜa Barqi al-Askari! How could you even approach her? As students at Higher Teachers' College, we did not dream we could one day tell her 'Good morning,' even from a distance . . ."

In those days I discovered the democracy in the teaching methods in Iraqi higher institutions, which had become accessible and were built on scientific principles of Iraqi professors who were specialists in education and psychology, most of whom had studied in the United States. They were disciples of the philosopher Dewey and his theories and were distinguished by their nationalist aspirations. However, the society by necessity moved more slowly than those idealists, for poverty had a concrete presence everywhere, and emigration from the countryside to the city did not always mean acquiring the spirit of the city's modernity overnight and becoming modern. I noticed that the young were increasingly interested in joining the colleges, particularly Higher Teachers' College; they sought diplomas that would secure them positions with a salary considered to be good in those days, for it was enough to save them from poverty and make it easy for them to get married, especially to spouses who were also university graduates and who could also be employed.

It was obvious that most of my male students wore old clothes and that they did not change them all year. They were from the working classes of the city and the country districts and were determined to continue their education whatever difficulties they faced. It was obvious that Iraq's educational system in those days made it possible for a boy who was born in a poor mud shack and who had spent his childhood barefooted to have the opportunity to complete his university education and even to earn a doctorate at any university in the world by being given a fellowship or grant if he showed evidence of intelligence and ability to persevere—all, without having to spend one fils of his own.

At the colleges, the men met women who were mostly of a higher social class because the relatively rich families were the ones who wanted their daughters to be educated and cultured, while the majority of the poor families were satisfied to give their daughters only some education in elementary schools, and perhaps rarely in secondary ones too—that is, if they did not keep them totally illiterate and uneducated. On the other hand, if the young men from wealthy families did not enter the College of Medicine in Baghdad, most continued their higher education in Beirut, Damascus, or Cairo—if not in England or America.

The Iraqi colleges were all coeducational with the exception of Queen Aliya College, which was established to educate the daughters of the well-to-do families who still insisted on remaining traditional and conservative and would not accept the mixing of the two sexes. It was abundantly clear in the colleges that the female students belonged mostly to comfortably affluent families, as was evident from the way they dressed and behaved and from their self-confidence vis-à-vis the poorer male students who had not yet been able to shed the signs of the primitive life, from which they came.

Although the administration of each of the colleges accepted democratic methods and the equality of all students, social class differences continued to make the mixing of the two sexes limited and difficult. The young women thus appeared to the young men as though they were in a faraway, dreamy universe difficult to reach. This created fertile ground for beautiful amatory poetry written by students of the various colleges in Baghdad from the middle of the 1940s until the end of the 1950s. This poetry spread fast in intellectual circles, whether it was published in the daily newspapers or not; and most of it was written by the students of the Higher Teachers' College and the College of Law, although the poetess Fatina al-Naib, one of my students at Queen Aliya College was also known for her poetry in those days, but she was older than all her fellow students by several years.

In addition to all this, a cultural effervescence was ascendant in the city in those days. It was an effervescence in which destinies mixed and enthusiasms took exciting and ever-changing political and social directions, and I found myself in its whirl perhaps at just the right historical moment. There were the young women who were itching for their freedom, and I knew many of them. There were the poets and short-story writers who were seeking to create new forms in everything they wrote. There were the painters who had returned from their study abroad and who, despite their small numbers, were able to create new theories for Arab art everywhere, out of the expression of their experiences in lines and colors. There were also the persons specializing in economic, social, political, philosophical, and historical thought, ranging from the extreme right to the extreme left. They were eminently represented by a number of professors, prominent in their colleges, who were no less influential than their friends the writers and artists in shedding the old traditions and announcing the good news of a forthcoming modernity that would change the whole Arab world, not only in relation to political and social attitudes but also with regard to the aspirations, visions, and emphatic call for freedom in all its forms that individual men and women were harboring in their hearts.

When the College of Arts and Sciences was in its second year, I was charged with organizing a season of cultural activities in accordance with the traditions of the other colleges. I depended on the college's professors themselves, and I gave them an open platform every week or two from which to speak to a broad audience in the Queen Aliya College's auditorium, whose big building was across that of the College of Arts. I chaired the meetings and introduced the speakers every time.

Among those who gave lectures was Dr. Albert Nasri Nadir, professor of philosophy. He spoke about existentialism, its philosophical roots, and Sartre's theorizations about it. Existentialism had then swept the universe of intellectuals with its magic fire, although many understood it wrongly. At the end of the lecture, the discussion was heated and long, and lasted more than two hours.

Dr. Ahmad Salih al-Ali, a professor of history, spoke about the financial affairs of the city of Basra in early Islamic history, and his lecture was precise and clever. As soon as he had finished and I asked the audience as usual to pose questions, a turbaned shaykh came forward to the platform; we later learned that he was Professor Muhammad al-Sawwaf. Without greeting the chairman of the meeting or asking permission, he launched a severe attack on the lecturer, almost accusing him of unbelief, speaking in a loud voice and using a harsh language we were not accustomed to on such intellectual occasions. I tried to calm him down and persuade him to soften his tone, while the audience was aghast . . .

Two weeks after that, Dr. Ali al-Wardi, professor of sociology, gave a lecture. He had recently returned from the United States, where he had earned a doctorate. His lecture was about the duality of the Iraqi personality, and it aroused a long and enjoyable discussion among the crowded listeners for about two hours. The newspapers on the next few days repeated much of the content of the lecture and the discussion; and with that began the fame of Dr. Ali al-Wardi, the like of which only a few of the university professors enjoyed in those days. He enjoyed a special popularity, which continued for more than thirty years, based on the articles and books he later wrote.

The audience of all these lectures consisted of mostly young men and women in amazingly large numbers. The auditorium could not seat everyone, and many remained standing. When the lectures ended, the people always left while engrossed in discussing with visible vigor what they had heard.

I naturally had my share in all that activity, apart from organizing and chairing the meetings. I gave a lecture entitled "Byron and Satanism" and was introduced to the audience by one of my colleagues. He highlighted my place in the writing of those days by saying that I wrote with a spirit unknown to our newspapers and magazines (as he said). I did not know whether my colleague knew that I had just arrived at the auditorium, situated at Bab al-Muazzam at the far north end of al-Rashid Street, from a hall at the far south end of the same street, namely the Hall of Ancient Fashions, situated at al-Bab al-Sharqi where I had attended the opening of the first exhibit of the Baghdad Modern Art Group. That was on April 21, 1951. Jawad Salim had insisted that I participate in that exhibit and show my oil paintings. I had resisted at first because I was a Palestinian and not a professional painter, but he himself came to my apartment to take the paintings in his small Fiat, and we worked hard along with Shakir Hasan, Qahtan Awni, and others to make it an eye-catching, noted exhibit.

One of my six paintings represented three village women from Palestine that I had painted in Bethlehem in the difficult days of 1948. The women in the painting were sitting on the ground in blue, green, and red robes around a basket of fruit and looked more like three goddesses of grandeur and eternal endurance; I had reworked the tableau by thickening its colors with the brush and the knife early in 1951.

Without our being aware of it at the time, this exhibit was destined to represent the beginning of a new stage in the history of Iraqi art. It was the beginning of modernism in Baghdad, not only in painting and sculpture and the writing and theorization about plastic arts that accompanied them but also in intellectual attitudes and styles that began to pervade verbal arts, first in Iraq and then in all the Arab world. The speech which Jawad Salim made at the opening of the exhibit was, in part, written by me especially for that occasion.*

In all these public activities, I was really interested in my friends, whom I saw and with whom I engaged in endless conversations almost every day. However, Lami⁣ᶜa became my greatest interest after our first meeting, but our circle was getting larger whether we liked it or not. We both tried to shrink it lest it should become impossible for us to be alone together, for we needed privacy in one way or another but did not always have it. All my friends were unmarried, and we met at first as a coterie; but attraction and repulsion between genders was inevitable and the group evolved into a loose assemblage of couples.

Now and then, Lamiᶜa invited us to her home for tea, and thus I got acquainted with her mother, a lady past fifty whose attitude and manner of speech gave the impression that, despite the death of her husband five years earlier, she had known wealth and luxury most of her life. The house was new, having been built less than a year before, and I liked its modern plan, which was different from the traditional ones that Baghdad's people were accustomed to until that time. It was designed by architect Hazim Namiq, a graduate of the University of Wales, and one of a small group of architects in Iraq whose members were known for having planned buildings for the government that were distinguished by their brave vision and design. Namiq's wife, Aliya al-Umari,

---

*For details concerning the role of Jawad Salim and the Baghdad Modern Art Group, see my book *Jawad Salim wa Nusb al-Hurriyya* (Jawad Salim and the Liberty Monument), published by the Ministry of Culture and Information, Baghdad, 1975.

had been like a sister to Lami^{c}a since their childhood in Mosul; she was even closer to her than any sister or brother all her life. I soon discovered that Aliya al-Umari was Lami^{c}a's only confidante; she kept her secrets and was her most important resource in all matters, whether emotional or otherwise. In those days, I was still alternating between serious and playful relationships with others and did not know as a Palestinian where my experience would lead me the next day. How was I to know the role that Aliya and her two brothers, and even all the al-Umari family with its wonderful members, men and women, would play in my life and in Lami^{c}a's? From those first obscure, anxious moments, they would prepare for us a psychological attachment, without which we would have been lost in harsh and unfair labyrinths?

At the first tea party that Lami^{c}a gave us in the garden of her home, there were four or five men and three women. Umm Amer—Lami^{c}a's mother—looked at her daughter's guests from the window as they drank tea and were being served by Umm Shakir and her son under Lami^{c}a's supervision. Suddenly—as Umm Amer later said to her daughter—she was startled when her eyes fell on me, not the others, as I was engaged in conversation, and her heart began to beat fast. A strange thought moved in her breast, and she wondered, "Who is this young man?" She opened the balcony door and, before coming to us, called Lami^{c}a to her, closed the door behind her, and asked her, "Who is that man?" pointing to me from the window. Lami^{c}a laughed and told her that I was one of her colleagues, like the other guests. Her mother said, "Why did my heart wince when I saw him?" Lami^{c}a understood her and responded, still laughing, "He is a stranger, mother, a Palestinian. Don't be afraid. He is also a Christian . . . Take it easy."

"Ah, you set my heart to rest," Umm Amer said, "may God set your heart to rest!" What always worried her, for some reason, was that Lami^{c}a would get married—attached to her daughter as she was and unable to imagine Lami^{c}a independent of her. What a strange insight Umm Amer had at that moment, when none of us was thinking of such a thing!

Lami'a returned to the garden with her mother and introduced us, one by one. Umm Amer knew some of us and took part in the conversation with the fluency of a lady who was confident of her distinguished social position. When painting and the making of portraits became the subject of the conversation, it was mentioned how a clever painter sometimes altered or even disfigured the features of the person being painted in order to seek stronger expression. When I said that I enjoyed drawing people with a pencil, Umm Amer suggested laughingly that I should draw Lami'a for her. I warmly responded to her suggestion, saying, "I will draw her and make her look like a bride!" Whereupon Umm Amer frowned at me and said, "May God's good omen prevail, not your foreboding. Draw her as she is and leave the brides to others."

∎ ∎ ∎

And, indeed, I left the brides to others, although only for a few months. As a result, I was afflicted with what I had experienced for a time in England when I was a student: loving two or more women at the same time without being able to free myself from any of them. The problem this time was that there were three, and each knew or suspected that, at the least, my affections were divided between her and another woman.

A dream, which I had dreamed several times in the middle 1940s when I was in Jerusalem, returned to me. I saw myself descending an endless spiral staircase. With me were two women, one was naked and the other dressed. Around us were crowds of people, of whom I saw only the faces. They all turned toward me, their eyes bulging and their mouths gaping. It seemed as if they were nothing but moving masks, ascending and descending the stairs; they all passed by me, and I paid no attention to them but continued to hug both women in complete harmony. During the dream, I was conscious of wondering, are we in the hall of a large theater, or are we gradually descending the stairs leading to hell? I finally painted this scene on a large canvas in 1946 in Jerusalem, not knowing what it meant—and I stopped having the dream. And here I was, five years later, seeing similar visions. The dream of the two women was repeated: again one was dressed and the other naked; and I was embracing both. The scene of the masks around me changed each time, and I was aware each time that I was wondering, are we in a large theater? Are we descending the stairs of the marble hall at the Opéra in Paris—which I had not yet visited at the time—or are we gradually descending into hell?

At a big celebration of one of the colleges held in King Faysal II Hall at Bab al-Muazzam, I was with a number of professors and students of the College of Arts, sitting on one of the seats of the parterre. The higher balconies were crowded with professors and students from various colleges. I noticed that Lami^ca was sitting in a box, glittering among her friends. I waved from my distant seat, and she returned my greeting with a wave and a big smile. A little while later, I noticed that my faithful female student was sitting in another box near hers—the boxes being open to one another—and she looked at me from above, gazing beautifully at me and making me turn my eyes repeatedly in her direction from time to time. I was not aware that, whenever I raised my eyes toward her, Lami^ca saw me looking in a compromising direction: here was her rival, separated from her only by a few seats, seeing me exchanging looks with her. Lami^ca turned away her eyes from me with an affected scorn, whenever I tried to draw her attention . . . And I realized what had happened.

At the end of the celebration, I made a point of hurrying out in order to meet Lami^ca. But as soon as I found her, she frowned, turned away from me, and walked away with her friend without a single word. I felt that the earth had split under my feet . . . Seconds later, my student arrived with a friend. She did not dare give me more than a passionately loving look and a discreet gesture of her hand that no one saw but me, heedless of whether I was waiting for Lami^ca or anyone else . . .

That night Lami^ca accused me of the ugliest things that lovers can accuse each other of. And I did not tell her about the dream of the two women, which haunted me every night when I went to sleep.

(2)

Wherever he went, Adnan Raouf attracted attention with his height, handsome face, and gentle and sympathetic disposition.

And ever since I read in manuscript form two or three of his short stories that had a distinct style and noticed his bold thinking so different from what was prevalent, I expected an imminent literary reputation for him, not only in Iraq but also in the rest of the Arab world. The Arab imagination at the time was at the beginning of a wonderful awakening, possessing the desire to realize what was new and authentic, and what would give the Arab nation hope for a future that could transcend the decadence it had endured for more than seven hundred years, and also surpass the achievements of the renaissance and enlightenment of the middle of the nineteenth century to the Second World War. That ambition was, no doubt, part of the bond that united Adnan and Buland al-Haydari who, as chance would have it, were neighbors on Taha Street. Buland was close to Adnan in age and daily ventured to write a poem the likes of which readers in Iraq had never seen.

And also as chance would have it, I was introduced to them both at Desmond Stewart's home at the beginning of 1949, when he invited me to dinner—we both being colleagues teaching English at Preparatory College. I arrived at his house in the al-Battawiyyin neighborhood where he had recently moved after living for two or three months in a hotel on the river front (while I was given a room with a bath at the college itself). On arriving, I found Desmond's roommate, Henry Baker, waiting for me, and he apologized for Desmond's absence. Henry said that he had gone out and was late to return for some reason but emphasized that he would be back shortly. When Desmond returned, he reiterated his friend's apology and was accompanied by two young Iraqi men—Buland and Adnan. They described how they met at Cinema Ghazi, known at the time to be one of the meeting places of Iraqi educated society. They had sat next to one another in the cinema, and as was Desmond's custom whenever he met strangers whose shape he liked, he apparently struck up a conversation with them. He was twenty-four years of age, a recent graduate of the University of Oxford. In a few minutes, they were engaged in conversation, interrupted only by watching the movie. Soon afterwards, Desmond said that he had a guest for dinner that evening, a colleague who was a writer in Arabic and English, and asked if they would accompany him home for dinner too. They immediately decided to leave the cinema before the end of the movie and walk to where I was waiting with Henry.

We got to know one another quickly and directly. As soon as they heard my name (which they had not made out from their host because he pronounced it badly in English), they said—or so they claimed—that they had heard of me and read some of my work. I myself had read some of Buland's poetry in *al-Adib,* the Lebanese monthly magazine. It turned out that Adnan was assiduously studying English on his own and was enjoying speaking it, while Buland was trying to conceal that he did know it well. When we left together at the end of the evening, we walked toward the bus station near Cinema Ghazi and realized that the three of us were taking the bus that went to al-Azamiyya and that they would get off at the station just before mine at Taha Street, for Preparatory College where I lived was at the beginning of al-Azamiyya. We discovered that Samira, Adnan's sister, and Afsar, Buland's sister, were both my students at college and were both outstanding. That was no wonder, for this college, which became the College of Arts and Sciences in the fall of that year, had about one hundred male and female students who had excelled in the latest matriculation examination, and we had to prepare them to go on scholarship to various universities in England and the United States by giving them extra advanced courses in English, Arabic, mathematics, and physics.

The afternoon of the next day, Adnan and Buland came to visit me at the college and thus began an intimate friendship that brought us together almost every evening if I had no appointment with others. We would spend much of our free time together, along with some other friends the number of whom soon increased, in my room or in the cafés on al-Rashid Street or on Abou Nuwas Street running along the Tigris, where hundreds of people walked every evening on the river bank or sat at the tea houses crowded with guests and domino players. Our conversations on poetry, the short story, painting, and sculpture never stopped but to start again in a sequence that knew no end.

I learned that Adnan had graduated from the College of Law the previous year, 1948, and was looking for a job . . . He was clearly ambitious and had considerable talents and capabilities, and he would later deservedly occupy important positions, first at the Iraq Petroleum Company, then at the Ministry of Foreign Affairs, and later at the United Nations.

As for Buland, I did not exactly know his academic background until I discovered that officially he was still a middle-high-school student at one of the national schools, although he was then over twenty-two years of age. However, and despite his clear intelligence and wide learning, he was not going to any school and did not have any regular position, because he did not care for school or college, especially after he had published his first collection, *Khafqat al-Tin* (The Throb of Clay), with its innovative poetic experiences, three years earlier. His only interest was loafing around as he liked in the streets of Baghdad in the company of Husayn Mirdan, in spite of the great difference in their social status. Husayn Mirdan was the son of a poor policeman in Baqouba and had run away to Baghdad to escape his father and his job of carrying clay and bricks at construction sites. On the other hand, Buland was the son of a high-ranking army officer (who was dead at the time I met Buland), and he belonged to a well-known Kurdish family in Baghdad, his grandfather having been Shaykh al-Islam in Istanbul, appointed by Sultan Abd al-Hamid. Buland was living at the time with his sister Roxane and her husband but was uncomfortable with that.

I liked this young man who resembled a Rimbaud in a time and place other than nineteenth-century France. Until the summer of that year, Buland wore a long raincoat, which he never took off to disclose the suit, doubtlessly old, that it covered . . . He had no income except for a few dinars he received monthly from his maternal uncle, general director of the Department of Agriculture, for proofreading the magazine published by the department. In spite of that, he talked and acted with pride and confidence as though his pockets were full of dinars, which he could spend right and left without limit.

The early 1950s for the young literati of Baghdad was the golden age of existentialism, whatever their understanding of it was from the translations of the writings of Jean-Paul Sartre and Albert Camus that reached them or from translated articles about them. Few of them could distinguish one from the other, and fewer still realized that Albert Camus was not an existentialist in the political or nonpolitical sense that Sartre meant. Most of them liked to understand existentialism as a new bohemianism, philosophized this time in the cafés of Saint-Germain in Paris. For some, it meant commitment as the left in those days understood it. There were some who saw in its logic something exactly the opposite, namely, a sort of nihilism that allowed the individual to go beyond all values and all political philosophies in cities that "boredom killed" or, in the words of Camus in his essay "A Stand in Oran," in cities which "the Minotaur devoured."

Buland al-Haydari, who considered himself an existentialist in those days, was taken by this idea in his rebellious way. Inspired by it, he wrote his few poems entitled "Aghani al-Madina al-Mayta" (Songs of the Dead City) in a pointed language of masterly simplicity that rejected the traditional rhetorical images and had its own musical rhythm and dramatic style. It also contained some images that had come to him early and spontaneously when he was a student in secondary school, and it had lots of the feeling of the curse that fascinated him in the poetry of Ilyas Abou Shabaka. I was enthused by these poems in 1949 as he brought them to me one by one, and we discussed them till they took their final form. Then I wrote an introduction to them entitled "al-Shiᶜr al-Jadid" (The New Poetry), and I made some pencil drawings for them. But he could not publish them until the summer of 1952, without the drawings.

His friend Husayn Mirdan was no less sensitive than Buland about all that. But at first he was hesitant to rebel against the tradition of poetic meters and the single rhyme throughout the poem as Buland had done. He wrote his first collection *Qasa'id*

Ariya (Naked Poems) in the traditional meters, saying with the pride and defiance of the cursèd poet, "I was suckled the milk of profligacy at my mother's breast." This laid him open to being arrested on charges of licentiousness because of his poetic collection, the "audacious" cover of which was drawn by Jawad Salim (who later also drew the cover of *Aghani al-Madina al-Mayta*). However, the judge was more intelligent than those who arrested Mirdan and more sympathetic to poets and poetry; for he asked Muhammad Mahdi al-Jawahiri to testify about Husayn Mirdan's collection, and the great poet did not hesitate to support its integrity as literature, the author of which deserved admiration, not being thrown in prison.

I was surprised when Husayn Mirdan gave me a copy of *Qasa'id Ariya* and wrote an inscription on the top of the first page that said, "To the genius . . ." I protested, saying, "Being thirty, and still a genius?" He said, "And why not? We are the new geniuses." In spite of his extreme poverty in those days and his vagabond and bankrupt life, he was greatly confident of his talent that no regular education had polished after he left his job in construction and clay. Two or three years later, he published another book, which he dedicated in large letters, "To the giant wrapped in the fog of time, Husayn Mirdan."

In the early 1950s, the young literati in Baghdad—and also in Beirut, Damascus, and Cairo—had a feeling that the new writings they had to come up with to enliven the spirit of a nation that was threatened from every direction gave them the right to impose their revolutionary intellectual quarrels on the current media of those days. They really believed in their different talents, although the media were few in relation to their larger numbers in later decades. They did not have to apologize to their predecessors and expected, even though they were still at the beginning of the road, that their achievements would make their generation the most important force in the psychological and intellectual change in Arab society.

There was a critic in Beirut, great on account of his importance and age, whose name was Maroun Abboud. He followed the writings of the young literati affectionately and precisely in the columns of the newspapers he wrote for, and he suggested to them that their creative impulses were legitimate. But most of them began to support or criticize one another, sometimes with much love and sometimes with no mean measure of boor-ishness. As a result they were in a state of constant preparedness, ready to defend their writings with all the strong arguments they had, with warmth and sometimes with anger. They were also ready to come up with poems, short stories, or critical essays, the originality of which always surprised their readers. From the middle of the 1940s to the end of the 1950s, it was clear that the great majority of these excited writers were students and gradu-ates of the Iraqi colleges of which there were only a few in those days. Everything these writers wrote had a strong echo outside Iraq too.

In the spring of 1951 and in such an atmosphere, I received a letter from one of these young men, a Syrian short-story writer I did not know personally, whose name was Ilyas Maqdisi Ilyas. In his letter, he "prophesied," after having read some of my articles and two or three of my short stories published in *al-Adib* of Beirut, that I would inevitably one day win the Nobel Prize for literature. Alas, he will remain waiting for that day!

■　■　■

Lami^ca and I had just finished having lunch at the Sindbad Hotel and were on our way out when I was surprised to see a familiar face coming toward me in the corridor. I could not believe that I was seeing Denys Johnson Davies, whom I had not seen since our days together in London in the fall of 1943. The last time we had corresponded, he was teaching translation at one of the universities in Cairo in 1946. He knew Arabic well, for he had studied it along with Persian at the University of Cambridge with Professor Arberry when I was studying English literature there. He had published in Cairo his translation of a collection of short stories by Mahmoud Taymour, which I had praised in a special article after reading it in Jerusalem. Here he was in front of me, slender, blond, and handsome. He wore an elegant, striped, dark blue suit. I had known him to wear nothing but simple, sport clothing during the period of rationing in England during the war.

I introduced him to Lami^c^a, and he was very pleased to meet her. I immediately remembered the day eight years earlier when I had introduced him to my English girlfriend Gladys Newby and he had introduced me to his Egyptian girlfriend Ijlal Hafiz, and I recalled our going to restaurants together many times.

"Have you come to Baghdad to teach?" I immediately asked.

"Not at all," he answered. "I'm here to do more important work than that . . . I'll tell you about it later."

Lami^c^a had to go home, so we left the hotel, she took a taxi, and I took my old friend to my apartment at the pension, which was at a distance of twenty steps or less. He began telling me about the task that brought him to Iraq. He had returned to London from Cairo and was lately able to find a job with De La Rue Company, which specialized in printing paper money for many governments of the world. Because he could speak Arabic well, he was put in charge of approaching the authorities in the Iraqi government in order to persuade them to leave the company that printed their money and move to De La Rue Company. He was wearing the expensive suit as part of the appearance that is necessary when one negotiates with officials on behalf of an important company. When dealing with Iraqi officials, he found out that they understood his Cairene dialect, but he did not understand their Baghdadi dialect. So both turned to Classical Arabic or English, which was understood by both. He stayed at the Semiramis Hotel and knew that I was in Baghdad from reading my work in Arabic magazines. He asked at the hotel about me, and they told him, "Ask about him in the nearby Sindbad Hotel." And so, we met again after many years of separation!

Two or three days later, Denys found out that he had to prolong his stay in Baghdad because those he was dealing with had apparently not given him a definitive answer regarding the matter he was consulting them about. I introduced him to Buland, Hilmi Samara, Abd al-Malik Nouri, and others. He decided to move to the much cheaper Arab League Hotel near King Faysal II Square, which was at a short distance from us. When the writ-

86

ers learned that he knew Arabic and was fond of translating short stories of Egyptian authors he knew personally like Tawfiq al-Hakim, Mahmoud Taymour, Najib Mahfouz, Yousuf al-Sharouni, and others, he found himself immersed in a strange sea of them . . . They used to come to see him early at the hotel, perhaps before he had gotten up from bed, the first among them usually being Husayn Mirdan. They sat with him most of the morning hours, while I was occupied lecturing at the colleges, and—as he said to me, both amused and surprised—they broached the strangest topics of conversation with him, not only literary ones but also political and social ones. They expected him not only to translate their works into English but also to support their causes abroad even though he knew nothing about them.

On the first Friday, we saved him from all that. Hilmi, Buland, and I took him in Dr. Hilmi's MG convertible, famous for its small size and red color, to Salman Pak, thirty kilometers to the south of Baghdad, to see Chosroes's palace built by the Sassanids in the fourth century AD and overrun by Saᶜd ibn Abi Waqqas at the Battle of Qadisiyya three centuries later. Its remains continue to suggest the magnificence of its ancient Iraqi architecture inspired by the Assyrian style that is distinguished by the large arch.

When we returned in the evening, we went to a folksy outdoor café on Abou Nuwas Street where I often went whenever I needed solitude as the Tigris River blazed with the reflections of the setting sun, the clouds brushing it with red, gold, and violet hues, a celebration of chaotic colors that was not often repeated in spring evenings anywhere else but in the sky of this wide river, full of movement and activity. On the river bank, those who broiled *mazqouf* (fish roasted on wooden stakes) were preparing for their beautiful task, as had been done daily for tens of centuries.

After supper, we went to my apartment. Moments later, Nizar Salim, accompanied by a friend or two, dropped in with his round, laughing face. Some of us sat on my wide bed, which was transformed in the daytime to an excellent sofa, some others sat on chairs, and others sat on cushions on the floor.

As we were engrossed in conversation, Nizar began to draw

us with a pencil, one by one. His drawings were caricatures that were among the best he had drawn, skillfully capturing the way each of us sat, gestured, and smoked. He drew Hilmi holding his curved pipe that was larger than the car he was driving, the car almost collapsing under him; his drawing of Denys suggested the latter's English delicacy as though he had just arrived from Bloomsbury in London; he drew me with the pipe in my hand, by which I was emphasizing what my features were saying; he drew Buland wandering aimlessly; and finally he drew himself with eyeglasses with two big lenses, underneath which was his sneering laugh.*

Denys was amazed at the rebellious, dashing spirit he observed in the artists and writers of Baghdad. When I showed him some of their short stories, he felt he had discovered a universe he, and his friends in Cairo, knew nothing about. (He later translated into English stories by Abd al-Malik Nouri, Fuad al-Takarli, and others in addition to three short stories of mine, and he published them in various magazines. Most of them finally found their way to his important book, *Modern Arabic Short Stories,* which the Oxford University Press published in the middle of the 1960s and which still remains one of the best sources of modern Arabic literature.)

One thing that amazed him was the constant talk about existentialism. The English are rarely taken by literary fashions, which the rest of Europeans—especially the French—are distinguished for. Existentialism itself had occupied a central place of interest among the writers of the world after the end of the Second World War and most of the 1950s, but it had not excited more than a mere academic curiosity among English writers in spite of the fame of Sartre, Camus, and Gabriel Marcel. Denys could not find any explanation for this interest in Baghdad, where people read the French only in translation, yet they found something that dazzled them and nourished their aspirations for the new and different.

One day he suggested a cunning plan to score a hit on our

---

*Nizar gave me these drawings as a gift. Several years later he borrowed them from me to show them at one of his exhibits, but he never returned them.

friend Buland. He said, "Write a strange poem, with very strange images, symbols, and language; and fill it with philosophical allusions and terms used frequently in the writings of the existentialists; and let us claim that you translated it from Sartre by way of English . . ."

So we sat together in my room, and I wrote the so-called poem and filled it with strange expressions, sometimes ones that Denys invented. That evening Buland, Najib al-Mani, and Zuhdi Jarallah came, and the landlady brought us tea. I then claimed that I had found a rare poem by Sartre translated into English in the latest issue of *Encounter* and that I had translated it into Arabic. Might I read it to them? They all agreed, so I took out the papers on which I had written the poem, but I was afraid that Najib al-Mani would expose the game, because he read English and regularly followed what appeared in *Encounter*.

> "The claws of night mangle
> The streets' torn-off fragments,
> And the windows are bleeding
> With eyes made of steel . . ."

I read what I had written, with some affected gruffness in my delivery. From time to time, I jumped to the "footnotes" at the bottom of the page to read the explanations that the "author" himself had given for some of the obscurities and the proper nouns mentioned in the text. Everyone listened with seriousness and deep concentration that made me feel that my words had an extraordinary effect, which began to move me involuntarily while I affected an "existential" gravity, hoping it would also move the listeners.

When I finished reading, there were a few seconds of silence, interrupted by Buland who said, "Beautiful. And strange, very strange."

Denys made a point of encouraging him by saying that when philosophy—especially existential philosophy—interfered with poetic creativity, it corrupted it because philosophy soared in intellectual space and yet claimed that it was concerned with the present moment and the sensual experience.

As for Najib al-Mani, he emphasized that all the arts' skillful formulations, particularly the art of poetry, were worthless if they were not supported by real thought.

Zuhdi objected because of the absence of music or the impossibility of its existence in this kind of verbal argument: where was poetry, then?

The conversation continued in this manner as Buland said nothing more than "No," "Yes," "Perhaps." Suddenly he uncovered a real sensibility that amazed me when he said, addressing me, "This poem is very strange, because it resembles your paintings. It is as though it comes out of your own tableaux. Its symbols, its details—I've seen them, or I've seen the likes of them in your paintings of the last two years."

I felt as if he had exposed the game and also that he had uncovered intellectual relationship that the images of the poem disclosed, especially when he added, "If this poem were an existential one, whatever meaning we want to give it, your paintings are then existential, perhaps without your knowing it . . ."

At that, I pretended to laugh. I put the papers away and changed the subject somehow, while Denys looked sidelong at me, smiling—neither a winner, nor a loser!

That night, after my friends had left, I went back to that poem and held it as if I was holding a genie who had duped me, who was offering me a gem that I had not known existed, and I began to demand that he hand over that gem to me . . .

It was here, in this heap of words. I had to do away with the nonsense in it, to throw away the intended dross and the saucy fabrications it had, in order to raise from the heap a real, serious work that I could call a poem. Until that day, whenever I wrote poetry, the words came to me in English. Here were the words, now coming to me in Arabic; and they were of a kind that Arab poets were not accustomed to—they were sharp, wounding, physical words:

> "Give me your feet, marble from hell,
> Carved by the chisels of fingers . . ."

Where was the music in this? Let the music of the bygone centuries go to hell! Here was music that was stronger and more wonderful! That was what I said.

That night, I deleted more than half of the fake poem. What remained of it was a truth that could not be ridiculed . . . I entitled the resulting poem "A Song for Mid-Century." It was a middle-of-a-century love song, replete with man's state of being torn—physically, spiritually, historically.

Two or three days later, I had the opportunity to be alone with Lami^ca, and I related to her our story with Buland. I read the poem in its final form to her, and she said, "Your love poetry is awesome! One who sees you and speaks to you would never believe that your apparent softness conceals all this awe . . ."

I said, "Here then is a poem of another kind for you."

I gave her a poem I had written in English, describing her splendid, little hands— two of the secrets of her charm—as well as her lips that resembled "a chalice made of carnelian, on which the god of love was carved fettered in chains . . ." She said, "Read it to me. I'd like to hear it in your voice . . ."

And that was the beginning of countless readings in coming days that she always wanted to hear in my own voice.

On the following day, I said to my students in their last year at Teachers' Training College, among whom were more than one poet and poetess, that I would read to them a new poem. They were excited by the idea, and lo, they heard a kind of poetry to which they were not accustomed:

> "Will I wake up every morning to see
> Tranquil eyes offered to me with breakfast
> And with bits of the sun chewed by winter's teeth?
> In your hair, there is jubilant silk,
> And in my hands, an ancient thirst; even if lies
> Always trickle from your lips
> With evil morning and sterile night . . ."

As I read, more than one student interrupted me and asked me to repeat a section so that they could write down these lines in their notebooks. I repeated it, then continued till the end of the poem.

Then followed a discussion on this kind of "free verse," which, one student said, shook his confidence in the value of much of the poetry that he read in those days . . . I was not unaware of the fact that they were students of English literature who read some modern English poetry, a fact that facilitated for them the understanding of this new attitude to poetry. From that class, a poet graduated three years earlier, Badr Shakir al-Sayyab; and shortly afterwards, another distinguished poet would graduate, Abd al-Wahid Lulua.

■ ■ ■

For the two months, or slightly more, since first meeting Lami͑a at the beginning of spring at the Olympic Club, I was divided psychologically, physically, and intellectually as I had never been in my whole life. There was Lami͑a's circle, her male and female friends who were now my closest friends too; and there was the circle of writers and painters, which hardly coincided with Lami͑a's but which I was also close to; and there were the professors, men and women, a circle that had become marginal for me despite my daily contact with it.

These circles, intersecting one another through me, kept me in a state of continuous movement, most of it in shared activities. My attachment to Lami͑a was quickly increasing, although I maintained other beautiful relationships I did not want to cut off. In the middle of all this, I had a feeling, which I did not want to discuss, that I was no more than a bird of passage and that all of this scene, although I loved it and was enlivened by it, was nothing but another Faustian experience on the way to knowledge, absolute knowledge, as a means to transcend the pain of being a stranger and an exile; and in my innermost soul, there were deep-seated sorrows about which I did not talk.

There was something unreal, yet more vivid to me than daily reality. It was as if I were writing a very strange poem as I was living it—even an extremely strange one this time. I did not care where it would lead me. Some of it put me in difficulties that might disturb me a little but that always excited me physically and spiritually. It blended tragedy with jest for me every day and finally transformed everything into a huge fantasy that would lead my imagination where I did not know.

(3)

The academic year usually ended a little after the first week of June. Mrs. Kazin Rashid, the assistant dean of Queen Aliya College came to see me at the beginning of May to talk about the art exhibit that the students put up every year before the year's final examinations and the beginning of the summer holidays. She had seen my works at the exhibit of the Baghdad Modern Art Group, so she asked me to participate in the college's exhibit, in one way or another, saying I owed that to the college!

When I showed her a collection of my line drawings, most of which dated back to the time I was in Jerusalem, she selected some of them and gave them to the students of the Manual Arts Department so that they might enlarge and copy them in color on canvas. Two or three students copied some of those drawings on ceramic vases fired in the electric kiln. All in all, their efforts resulted in beautiful works that would not have occurred to me, had it not been for these attempts. On that occasion, I took risks and drew ornamental motifs that were based on women's faces and flowers, stylized in my own way, and for the first time I painted on pottery specially prepared for me. All these were shown at the annual art exhibit, after I had made it a condition to Mrs. Kazin that my name should not be mentioned on them.

However, Kazin had insisted that I should also exhibit three or four oil paintings in my name, so I did. One I had painted in 1947 in Jerusalem; I was very fond and proud of it and carried it with me wherever I traveled. Its title was *The Woman Who Dreamt She Was the Sea*: it was a blue tableau, the color of the waves, and it represented an essay I had written in English some years earlier in a collection of essays entitled *The Annals of Love*. One of my students, Bakr Abbas (the younger brother of Ihsan Abbas), liked it very much and translated it into Arabic. I revised its rendering and published the greater part of it in *al-Adib,* a year or more before the exhibit, under the title "From the Record of Love and Death."

Mrs. Kazin knew that I never sold my paintings because I insisted on keeping them, no matter how many I accumulated. But she offered to buy this painting at whatever price I liked, and she insisted and repeated her offer twice, then thrice. I respected her and had a special affection for her, for she was a woman in her late thirties, distinguished by her fresh rosy complexion, her education and wide knowledge, and her fluency in English and French in addition to Arabic and Turkish. She loved life and pursued it with warmth and passion. I had no recourse but to weaken at her insistence, so I gave the tableau to her as a gift because she said she had fallen in love with it.

She invited me to a dinner party in the gardens of the Alawiyya Club. This club had been an English institution since the 1920s; only the English and other foreigners could belong to it. As for Iraqis, they were not permitted to become members unless they were ministers or former ministers or from the ruling families and influential elite of the country. Most of the servants and waiters in it were polite Athourians, modern-day descendents of the ancient Assyrians, known for their perfect service and discretion. They spoke Arabic with some difficulty and with a characteristic heavy accent, and they also spoke a kind of limited English with which they managed their affairs (there would come a time ten years later when the club would be Iraqized, but would still continue to be the distinguished social meeting place in town par excellence).

The evening was hot, but the garden was cool, with its lawn freshly mowed, sprinkled, elegantly manicured, and surrounded by rose bushes and dense bougainvillea. Our party included eight persons, including our hostess and her husband, who was a former minister, and we sat at a table on the edge of the garden.

I noticed that Mrs. Kazin, sitting at the head of the table opposite her husband, had seated me on her right, suggesting that I was the guest of honor. Apart from our hostess, there were two other elegant ladies, and I noted that the four men among my friends at dinner wore long-sleeved white shirts and neck-ties, while I had come wearing a short-sleeved blue shirt with an open neck—and no necktie. I suddenly realized that I had committed a big faux pas because the regulations of the club required men to wear a suit and a necktie in the evening; but if it was necessary to take off one's jacket because of the hot weather, it was required that one should wear a long-sleeved white shirt and a necktie.

I whispered in the hostess's ear, "I hope you'll excuse me, for I'm not dressed as I should be here . . ."

She answered me whispering and laughing, trying not to attract the others' attention, "Sargon, the waiter, came to me and drew my attention to that, while you were engaged in con-versation. I said to him in a low voice, 'Please, don't bring up this matter with my guest. He is a VIP . . .'"

I laughed and said, *"Pour épater les bourgeois."**

She responded, "You never spare any effort to do that, to judge from what I've observed of your conduct at the college, especially when you wore a necktie around your waist instead of a belt!"

She chuckled as she inserted a cigarette in her long cigarette holder, and I lit it.

■ ■ ■

Attendance at the college exhibit was great, and it contin-ued from morning to evening. I noticed that many young men had come to it because it was held at a girls' college, and they liked to talk to the female students who stood by the exhibits. The most attractive of them all was my student Mrs. Fatina al-Naib (who was older than I, being in her thirties, for she had joined the college after a long interruption of her studies and was the only student I allowed to smoke in class during lec-tures). She had earned a reputation for her love poems, which many learned by heart. This was a good opportunity for her admirers to see her without the black cloak she had to wear when she went outdoors among people. She had applied heavy

---

*To shock the traditionalists.

kohl to her eyelids, which gave her eyes an amazing brilliance, and she was ever ready to talk and laugh with the visitors.

Next morning, I met two visitors to the exhibit to whom I was introduced with pride by Mrs. Kazin: Mrs. Ismat al-Said, wife of Sabah Nouri al-Said, and Mrs. Suad al-Umari, wife of Mumtaz al-Umari, general director at the Ministry of the Interior, and daughter of Arshad al-Umari, a famous man who had been prime minister of Iraq more than once. Lami^ca had always talked to me about Suad with special admiration: and here she was, at the beginning of her thirties as I later learned, worthy of all the praise I had heard about her. Despite her young age, she was president of the Red Crescent Society; and her beauty, elegance, and conversation attracted people's attention. Her tall, slim figure combined tenderness and pride; and her conversation, whether she spoke in Arabic or English, suggested intelligence and knowledge. It appeared to me that she had heard about me from Lami^ca, and this was an opportunity for us to become acquainted. She focused on my paintings and Mrs. Kazin boasted to her that I had given her *The Woman Who Dreamt She Was the Sea* as a gift. We had a long conversation as we sipped the coffee that we were offered; and, most probably, Suad had had sufficient time to form an opinion of me, for she was not only Lami^ca's friend but also Aliya's sister-in-law, and Aliya was almost a twin sister to Lami^ca. Our meeting was the beginning of a family relationship that I did not foresee. (I will never forget that, after several months and many family meetings, I said to her one day in admiration of her articulateness and patriotism, "If this country were a republic, I would be the first to nominate you for its presidency.")

A few days later, a number of friends and I were visiting Lami^ca at her home when she said, "So, you've met Suad, haven't you? She is a great woman, don't you agree? But do you know what she said about you?"

I asked, "Has she said anything of importance?"

She answered, "I asked her what she thought of you and she said, 'I can't decide whether he is a real person or an artificial, unreal one . . .' And who can argue with Suad about her opinion?!"

"And you, what do you think? Am I real or unreal?"

"Very real, and this is my problem! But why didn't you tell me that you gave up a painting that you claim you love so much? To whom did you give *The Woman Who Dreamt She Was the Sea*? And just like that, for nothing?"

"So, you've heard?"

"Yes, and I want you to take it back."

"Impossible!"

"I'm angry . . . I want the painting."

I was under the impression that she had such a strong position with me or that I had such a strong position with her that she could command and demand. Signs of love between us were clear, however much we pretended to deny them and believe that what we had going on between us was only an intimate friendship hovering on the edge of love.

I said, "I'll paint other paintings for you. Tomorrow I'll bring you one I've recently painted."

She insisted that she wanted *The Woman Who Dreamt She Was the Sea*, although she would welcome having any other painting too. Suddenly and for the first time in my life, it occurred to me that I could paint, once more, the painting she wanted, although before that moment I felt that I could never do such a thing; painting one painting twice was an intolerable blasphemy in my view. But for Lami^ca? . . .

I said, "I will repaint it, only for you."

"And as it is exactly . . . When?"

"Please, don't hurry me. But I promise I'll paint it again. This will be the first and last time in my life that I will paint the same painting twice."

"Fine. I accept. And don't think I'll forget!"

Neither did she nor did I, but I procrastinated for several months until, one day, I took a painting that I had painted on plywood earlier. It represented my dear female student on the right side of the picture, facing the young man she loved on the other side. He was approaching her with his hand stretched out toward her (and what a beautiful hand I had made, with wonderful fingers!). He reached across a rocky Palestinian hill. I had later added a fearful, frowning face on the rock separating them; perhaps it was the face of the swordsman of the tales of *One Thousand and One Nights*—and he spoiled the whole picture . . . I now turned it over and on its back, I repainted *The Woman Who Dreamt She Was the Sea* with clouds swirling in the sky in the forms of beasts hovering around the woman. This was the spring of the next year. None of the painting's suggestions escaped Lami‘a, for they were apparently projected again and again to the surface from her deep unconscious, as from the depths of the sea, to vanish with the froth of the waves again and again.

■ ■ ■

The academic year was about to end, and I had decided to realize a wish that had been burning within me for years: to go to Paris and spend the months of the summer holidays there. This was now possible because at the end of May the college paid us our salary in one lump sum for the summer months.

If the money was available, the easiest thing in those days was to arrange a cruise by sea from Beirut to Marseilles and from there to Paris by train. The arrangements could be made through the Thomas Cook Company, whose office was next to the Sindbad Hotel, a few steps from my apartment. The person in charge there was a polite young man with a radiant face, whose name was Samuel. He arranged all the details for me and chose a Greek ship that stopped at several Mediterranean ports on its way to its destination: from Beirut, it sailed to Alexandria, and hence to Piraeus—Athens's port; it then visited Naples and headed for Marseilles, from which a trip to Paris by train was also arranged.

I was envied and considered fortunate by my friends who would remain behind and endure the blazing summer heat in Baghdad, which, in those days, had no cooling other than fans that blew hot air on you when the temperature was 48° C in the shade. Cooling systems were not yet known, although they became prevalent in Iraq some years later in an amazing fashion. As for air conditioning, it was nonexistent except perhaps in the homes of a very small number of wealthy people. But relief, or at least some respite, was possible in the pleasant midnight air, when people in thousands still filled the outdoor cafés on the banks of the Tigris or slept on the roofs of their homes, sprinkling the tiles with water at intervals.

Lamiᶜa and her friends, as well as my faithful female student, were not enthusiastic about my absence for such a long time. But they appreciated my having the opportunity to spend a whole summer in Paris. I promised I would write them now and then, until I returned to Baghdad at the beginning of October, loaded with Sindbadian reports and stories.

One afternoon before leaving, I was at Lamiᶜa's home. We sat on the elegantly cushioned settee near the wide back window of the main hall, which had become our preferred place. On its threshold, she had planted a green plant, perhaps a kind of basil rare in Baghdad, and it appeared to exhibit some dispirited weakness induced by the beginning of the summer heat. Lamiᶜa drew my attention to the plant and said, "Oh, who will enliven it?"

"This is the lovers' plant," I said, laughing. "Only sighs will enliven it . . . Do you water it every day?"

"Of course."

"Giving it water will do it no good. You should water it with tears . . ."

"Fine, I'll water it with tears."

"And when I return . . ."

"You'll find that it has grown and spread all over the window with my tears and sighs."

"And add to them also my own tears and sighs, will you?"

We often referred to it as the lovers' plant in later years, as it demanded our tears and sighs. It represented the great happiness that Lamiᶜa and I experienced, in spite of all the unrelenting crises and difficulties of life that the circumstances of history presented us.

(4)

As soon as I arrived in Beirut, I contacted a dear friend I had known since the time I lived in Jerusalem, Theo Tawfiq Kanan.

He had established a civil engineering office that had quickly become famous for its modern designs. Associated with him in establishing the office was another friend of mine, Asim Salam, who had returned from Cambridge, where he had attended my college, Fitzwilliam House, through my special intercession with its dean, William Thatcher. Theo's office was distinguished by a big mobile by Alexander Calder, the creator of this kind of sculpture. Suspended from the ceiling, it moved with the least touch or breeze, giving the place an extraordinary atmosphere of splendor.

Theo took me to his home in Ayn al-Murayyisa, descending with me to an old building that was level with the sea. He had restored the house and modernized its interior, keeping its large arched window that was built on the very rocks of the seaside. I spent three days with him, during which we contemplated the waves crashing on the window as they did in the distant perspective of stone houses evocative of ancient castles. We both spoke continuously about everything between heaven and earth, including Palestine, Jerusalem, his home in al-Musrara neighborhood, and mine in al-Qatamon, where we had last met four years earlier. On that day, the summer sun flooding his veranda induced in Theo a kind of ecstasy, and he suddenly took off his jacket and shirt to absorb that life-giving warmth and divine brilliance with the bare upper half of his body.

We were joined by his neighbor, Elie Bayt-Jali, who jumped from the rocks surrounding his home to those of Theo's . . . He read me two or three short stories he had written in English that were among the strangest I had ever heard. Without embarrassment, we all tried to revivify our wonderful days of Jerusalem, as though they had become memories of a paradise that no human feet would tread again.

The next day, I made an oil painting of the sea as seen through the window, and I focused on the distant stone houses, which formed one of the most wonderful scenes one would ever see on the shores of Beirut, or even all Lebanon.

I said, "Theo, look at that drift which the waves toss around . . . We, the Palestinians, are now like that, tossed by the world's waves, which bring us so close to one another that we can embrace, then separate us with their violence so that we fly off in a thousand directions. And we don't know if they will one day unite us again, even with their violence."

Before leaving Beirut, I wrote a long letter to Lamiᶜa, which was my first letter to her. I wrote another letter to my faithful female student, and I asked Theo to mail the two letters.

After I boarded the ship, I never saw Theo again. In the summer of the following year, he was visiting the archaeological remains of Jarash in Jordan when the stones of one site collapsed under his feet and killed him . . .

■ ■ ■

I will not speak about the details of my cruise, for it is another long story that is a bright thread in the fabric of my experiences that year, but that I must put aside, even for a while, in order not to stray too far from the more beautiful and resplendent thread in this fabric. The important thing was that, wherever the ship went and in whatever port it stopped for us to land and see the people, the markets, and the sites, Lamiᶜa always accompanied me—along with all the ship's young male and female passengers —in a manner I did not expect. But in my company too was my faithful female student, crowding out boisterous laughing Lamiᶜa with a strange silence resembling that of Byzantine icons. So I wrote a letter to each of them, which I mailed at the next port on our cruise.

I struck up a friendship with several passengers on board the ship. Among them was a young Egyptian man about my age, affable and shy, sent by his father to spend a month in Paris as a tourist to acquire some culture. He did not know any French, whereas I, for some months earlier in Baghdad, had studied French by myself and completed one or two parts of *Teach Yourself French*. In the beginning we stayed at the same hotel in Paris. The first thing that occurred to my friend was to go in the evening to the Folies Bergères show, so we went. The next evening, we went looking for a night club in Pigalle. In both cases, the naked women in their various poses and with their exciting enticements bored me, for in those places I could not find the beauty and allure of the two women who in my imagination continued to consume me. On the third day, some relatives of my friend came and took him out of the hotel. In the afternoon, I was surprised by a visit of a female friend of mine, who had also come from Baghdad to spend the summer in Paris and who wanted to apply for admission to the doctoral program at the Sorbonne.

One of my colleagues at the College of Arts and Sciences was a French professor called Monsieur Toupilier, who taught French literature and whose wife taught French at Queen Aliya College. They were both pleased that I had decided to travel to France, and they gave me the telephone number at their home in one of the suburbs of Paris. The first thing I did was to inform them of my arrival in Paris, where they too had just arrived. Two or three days later, they came to visit me and to help me move from my hotel in order to live with a French family, whose members would teach me to speak French, in addition to the fact that living with them would cost me much less than living in any hotel.

Looking at me through his big, thick eyeglasses, Monsieur Toupilier said, smiling cunningly, "You're an Arab, a Palestinian. Aren't you?"

I said, "Yes."

He said, "But you speak English so well, as you now do with me, that all who don't know you think you're an Englishman— an Englishman from Oxford or Cambridge."

I laughed, "Of course. I studied in Cambridge."

"Do you have any objection to pretending you're an Englishman?"

I did not understand what he meant, so he explained, "I know a very good French family, who lives on Boulevard Raspail, a neighborhood—as you know—that is nearly aristocratic. They have a room for rent, but only to an Englishman."

"Why to an Englishman, excluding all other human beings?"

"It's a womanly fantasy, my dear sir. The lady of the house is a widow who studied some English literature at one time before the war. She likes to speak English but cannot always find someone to speak it with, and she's afraid she'll forget the language. Worse still, her daughter is a student who is studying English literature too . . . Do you understand now?"

I said, "Sorry. I can't claim to be what you want me to."

He said, "You've nothing to worry about. I'll tell her what I want, and you've nothing to claim . . . You have only to speak English with the lady."

"But I want to live with a French family in order to practice my French, and you're asking me to do the contrary!"

"Not at all. Speak French whenever you want, although you'll find it difficult in the first weeks. But remember, my dear friend, that you're in Paris and French is still the language of Paris, in spite of the American invasion! You'll find that this family will give you a room in their beautiful house at an incredible rent that would never have occurred to you. Paris is not a cheap city to live in. Leave matters to me."

On the next day, Toupilier and his wife came and asked me to pack my bags and pay my hotel bill. I did and we went by taxi to Boulevard Raspail about which I had read. We entered a big building with many floors and went up to the second floor. We rang the bell at one of the doors, and a woman of about fifty came out. My two friends introduced me to her, and she welcomed me in French, but going along with my friend's plan and seeking to make things easy for myself, I spoke in English. The lady was pleased and called her daughter, whose face was covered with a white cream, perhaps because she had acne, and it looked like Harlequin's mask. They led me to a large room overlooking the main street. It had a small refrigerator, a wide bed, a sofa, two armchairs, a straight-backed chair, and a table. Could I ask for more than that? And the rent? I could not believe what I heard! It was exactly half of what I paid in Baghdad! The refined lady said, "As for breakfast, you have only to buy eggs, ham, butter, jam, bread, and coffee and I'll prepare breakfast for you every morning . . ."

I went downstairs to the street with Toupilier and his wife to tell them goodbye, and I wanted to be sure that he had not made me wear a mask I did not want. "Not at all, not at all," he said. "The lady did not ask me about your nationality because, as soon as she heard you spoke English, she forgot everything else!"

And so, that was what happened. The lady of the house helped me by answering my questions with precise detail. I had bought a good map of Paris and a Hachette tourist guidebook, as I always did later whenever I visited a large city I did not know; and so I located places and addresses on the map. I ventured and took the Métro, and I found it very much different from the Underground in London; but its plan was clear too, in its own way. Two or three days later, I joined the school of the Alliance Française, which was fortunately on the bus line that passed by the house, and so my mornings were mostly devoted to studying French there.

On my first day, the lady directed me to the *poste restante* in the city, where I had told Lami^{c}a and my faithful female student to send their letters until I informed them of my address. I found two letters waiting for me there—a long one from Lami^{c}a and another no less long from my student—as well as a third letter from my brother Yousuf in Bethlehem. We all exchanged letters continually during my stay in Paris.

It occurred to me to telephone one of the two young French women I had befriended on the ship. One was named Nadine and had given me her telephone number and said she lived in the suburbs. She came early next morning and took me out on what she called a tourist's visit to the city that she hardly knew herself. We went to the Champs Elysées and sat at a sidewalk café and drank coffee; then we went to the Arc de Triomphe in the middle of the famous Etoile; we went up into the Arc to its roof to see from its height how twelve wide avenues met at the Etoile. She told me with much pride about the person who planned them, and in whose honor the Arc de Triomphe was built and in what year. After lunch, we went to the Trocadéro square and came down the wide steps leading from it to the base of the Tour Eiffel. With hundreds of tourists, we went up in its large elevator to the first floor, then the second, then the topmost, the Tour being three hundred meters (about one thousand feet) above the roofs of the city. Since its erection in 1889, it has become the symbol of Paris, and no wonder, because until 1930 it had been the tallest structure in the world, and one of the miracles of mechanical engineering. Finally we went to a café and drank more coffee. Then I accompanied the young lady to the Métro and had the feeling that she was a very nice person, yet very inexperienced, one day with her being enough to exhaust all her talents.

I don't think I was ever as active and busy as I was during those three months in Paris—and I used to think I was very active in Baghdad! I was in constant movement in Paris, satisfying my ravenous appetite for culture, after years of hunger since I left Cambridge. I was beginning to feel that I was replenishing an intellectual store that had been exhausted in Baghdad. And here was the city that could provide nourishment, as much as you could take and devour. After an age of deprivation, how wonderful it was to go again to the theater, to the opera, and to concerts to hear Bach—not from scratched records, but live from pulsating musical instruments—and to follow delicate hands moving bows on violin strings with the grace and rhythm of dancers as they played the "Prelude" and "Fugue." And how wonderful it was to see rows of books on shelves and on the sidewalks!

When I went to the Louvre for the first time and wandered its halls, floor after floor, I felt a strange, delicious dizziness overtake me. All that I had studied on my own about art in books, from the earliest civilizations to the latest movement in painting and sculpture—I found it here in these thousands of real paintings and real statues, tempting me always to touch them as though they would respond as someone beloved would. I felt these sensations first at the Louvre, then at many other exhibits. After my second visit to the Louvre, I decided to ration all this extravagant wealth by visiting only one specific section every day or two, to focus on it while carrying a catalog containing details, names, and dates. In this way, I came to see all the exhibited items of the Louvre with an impossible rationality in the following weeks.

When I went to the Tuileries gardens to visit the Musée de l'Orangerie where the paintings of the Impressionists and the

Postimpressionists are kept, I experienced an overwhelming joy that shook me to the marrow! And true to my nature whenever I am surprised by beauty, I sighed and my eyes welled up, as I tried desperately to suppress my tears lest the visitors should see me and wonder why I was weeping! This was my state when, for the first time, I saw the paintings of Monet, Degas, Renoir, Pissarro, Sisley, Cézanne, Van Gogh, and the others—I saw them in their actual colors and sizes. And Van Gogh— his thick paint that looked as if he had just applied the bold strokes of yellow, blue, and green to the canvas with his wide brush electrified me, and, through the tremors of his madness, he communicated to me the achievement of a genius that, when it gets hold of the artist, multiplies his powers by one thousand and drains him, leaving him with nothing left but to die, out of love or out of pain for what his eyes have seen, what his hand has done, and what his heart has seized upon and treasured.

I went around, looking for the works of artists whose pictures and visions had haunted me since the days of my studies at Cambridge. My college stood opposite the Fitzwilliam Museum, which continued despite the war to offer exhibits that made me sometimes feel I was living with those artists as much as I lived with the geniuses of seventeenth-, eighteenth-, and nineteenth-century poets, novelists, and critics I studied, who had indefatigably persisted in enriching man's experience, indeed all humankind's civilization. Georges Braque's works gave me ecstasy, and when I saw him one day sauntering near his paintings, I was surprised on seeing both the awe he inspired and the simplicity he exhibited, and I thought: Such are those who change our times so that we may have more love and joy in an age corroded by the fear of a forthcoming nuclear war . . .

When I found an exhibit showing the works of Matisse, who was still alive at the time, I felt life redoubling in my veins and that I myself was increasingly responding to sensual beauty, without which living did not deserve to be called life. And when I saw Fernand Léger's paintings, with his workers going up and down scaffolds and turning with the gyrating wheels, as they spread bright blue love on everything that their hands made, spiraling up around it with their legs, while their faces exuded playful health as though the city was a circus with endless, exciting buffooneries—how I loved him and how often I returned to his paintings!

I returned to my room on Boulevard Raspail full of ecstasy, my hands trembling with longing for the brush, and I painted on paper with oil paints or made drawings with pencil. Since the time I had first gone to Baghdad, I painted on paper and sometimes on pieces of plywood, choosing small sizes of the latter because I knew that I had to move about with my paintings wherever I went and that large paintings were difficult for me to carry. I always had a feeling that, however strongly I imagined I was going to stay in a certain city, I was bound to leave it and had always to prepare myself for a forthcoming move.

Most evenings, I made it a habit to eat a simple supper in my room, of lettuce, tomatoes, celery, and some kinds of French cheese that I had become fond of—Camembert, Roquefort, and Brie—along with a French baguette, which one was almost content to make a meal of itself, let alone when it was buttered and accompanied by cheese.

All this gave me more eagerness, more energy, more desire to revel in the beauty of the experience of the eyes and the senses, which are tightly interwoven with the body and the intellect.

I continued my French lessons at the Alliance Française and wrote letters to Lami^ca and to my student. The lady from Baghdad who was applying to the Sorbonne visited me once or twice a week in afternoons of passionate love that carried me and her away perilously into chasms of the body's insanity, from which I did not find a way out for myself . . . I frequented the cafés of Saint Germain, knowing their names from what I read about the existentialists, and it seemed to me that I saw Jean-Paul Sartre once or twice at Café aux Deux Magots, although I always said that I was not interested in seeing contemporary great men. My fascination with Sartre himself had been quickly transcended by Albert Camus and André Malraux. (Five years later, I coincidentally saw the poet I loved, Louis MacNeice, to whom the English critic Reggie Smith often compared me when I used to write English poetry in Jerusalem. I saw him in London, sitting by himself at a sidewalk café in Upper Regent Street, and Tawfiq Sayigh was with me. We were both amazed at the physical resemblance between MacNeice and me, although his long hair had turned gray at the time, while I did not yet have a single white hair. That was the only time in my life when I almost rushed toward a man whose poetry had charmed me. And yet I refrained from doing so and remained with my friend, looking at MacNeice from a distance as he drank his coffee alone, until he left. A great regret and a deep sorrow came over me suddenly because I had not instantly rushed to pay for his coffee . . .)

Lamiᶜa's letters resembled her conversation: she joked and was merry, and I did not know sometimes whether she was serious or jesting in what she said or wrote. I always imagined I heard her silvery laughter. She spoke about the plant that she continued to water with her tears and to care for with her sighs. Her words reminded me of the songs she had taught me to love in Baghdad, some of which were in Arabic, some in an old Iraqi dialect, and some were songs popular in America in those days, especially those of Rosemary Clooney. I always felt Lamiᶜa's presence with me, laughing, boisterous, singing short segments of her favorite songs, then saying to me, "Come on, read me one of your poems." Or she would bring me Shakespeare's *Sonnets,* open the book at random, and say, "Read this sonnet to me, in your own voice and in your own way . . ."

But I also felt my dear student's presence too. She sent me long letters full of poetic fragments in Arabic and English, and I could not forget her. The Baghdad lady, who had come to follow up her registration at the Sorbonne University for a doctorate in French literature, her exciting physical presence was always with me too and she wanted me to forget all women but her.

One day, I received a letter from a fourth young woman from Bethlehem, who had completely slipped my mind. She said that she had gotten my Paris address from my brother Yousuf and that she was waiting for my return to the homeland . . .

I drew in pencil a picture of four women, interlacing before me as I looked from one to the other, while the female figure of a goddess that was so close to me as to be part of me whispered,

"Will you never make your choice? Will it be this one? That one? Me?" But their faces were all approximate copies of Lami^c a's face. Had this woman, whose love perplexed me, become all women to me?

The dreams about the two women whom I embraced in my sleep returned to me again, one woman was naked and the other clothed. We descended the endless spiral staircase together, among crowds of people amazed at what they saw. I had to get rid of this dream by somehow making a painting of this scene. I painted a handsome man, who heeded nothing and no one, and who tightly held to his chest the naked woman with his right arm and the clothed one with his left; they all walked in a street resembling Paris's, the three of them carrying many masks of every kind, suspended by strings from their hands and arms. From the balconies of the buildings around them, men and women looked down wearing masks as though they had just bought them from my three figures . . ."Mask Sellers," that was what I called the painting, for the artist often has many masks because it is his fate to live more than one life and to live more intensely than others. Every art work he creates is a mask that he has worn in one of his other lives and that he offers to others to wear in hours of their rich experiences.

Out of the many "facets" of reality, the artist makes "faces" for others that they need. I remember that in our childhood we called masks "faces." It gave us pleasure to wear many kinds of them, some were comical, others tragic, and others horrifying. I felt that the faces that the artist prepares for others to live by in his art work were much more varied, abundantly more comic, tragic, and horrifying, and very different from the trivial masks that society imposes on human beings every day. They are in need of the masks of the artist deep inside, where they act endless roles that they are afraid someone may see on their faces. It is easy for them to wear the mask of the external present moment and to take it off. As for the internal masks, the masks of the imagination, they are the ones they constantly search for and the ones they buy wherever they find them. The creative artists are their sources and their saviors.

In my painting, therefore, no one was without a mask except

the man and his two women. There would come a time in less than a year when I would find someone reminding me that he who walked without a mask among people, as did the figures in my painting, had to pay a high price.

Perhaps my thinking of masks was what revived in me a doubt that I had forgotten. A few days before leaving Paris, I said to the lady of the house as she entered my room, as every morning, with the breakfast she had prepared, "Madam, I'm very happy with the care you give me in such a beautiful manner. But I have a point I'd like to clarify."

"Yes? What is it?" she asked.

"Do you think I'm an Englishman?" I asked.

She appeared surprised. "I've never thought of the matter," she said. "The important thing is that my daughter Claudine and I are very happy with your presence with us."

I said, "I'm an Arab, a Palestinian. Do you know that?"

She arched her eyebrows a little and said, "Why not? It pleases me to know that we now have a friend who is an Arab, a Palestinian—and from Baghdad, too—who has stayed with us. Please, eat your breakfast."

I said, "My friend, Monsieur Toupilier . . ."

She interrupted me as she raised the cover off the plate with the two fried eggs, "Oh, Monsieur Toupilier is a dear friend and has not visited us for several weeks. He is a little strange. Don't you think so? But we like him and respect him. Then I'd like to tell you that when you return to Paris next summer, you should remember that we will be waiting for you. I'll prepare this very room for you, and I'll get some new furniture for you . . . How do you like my English language these days?"

"It's wonderful!" I said. "Next summer, I'll see whether you've kept it up at this level."

But I did not return to Paris "next summer."

In fact, I returned to Paris only thirty years later, in 1981. I visited Paris repeatedly all through the 1980s, but I had lost track of that gracious lady, the lady of the house on Boulevard Raspail.

■   ■   ■

In the middle of September, I went to the train station to take the train that would take me from Paris to Marseilles, and from there I would go by steamship to Beirut. Lo and behold, the Baghdad lady had made arrangements to see me, and I found her waiting for me at the station as I was looking for the sleeping car I had reserved for my night trip.

In order to bid me farewell the night before, she had invited me to a dinner she arranged, and she said she hoped I would not object, so I had accepted and said, "Not at all, even if dinner is only a sandwich we eat while walking." I was therefore surprised when she took me to a restaurant called Tour d'Argent, perhaps the absolutely most magnificent restaurant in Paris. In my financial situation at that time, I never dreamed of setting foot on its threshold, let alone going beyond it into that restaurant. Before every course, a different waiter came to describe the delicious foods you could choose or not choose; then another waiter came wearing a leather apron to suggest to you the wine that would go with the dish you had chosen; he would bring you the wine from the depths of his cellar stocked with old mellowed wines and suggest that you visit the cellar if you wanted—as I did. The waiter changed with every new course, and so did the wine in the darkened, luxurious setting made for the gourmet and promising him pleasure and sin . . .

There, on the train's platform, stood a woman at her beautiful best, who felt that this meeting would be our last, although she would return to Baghdad in one or two months. There were big tears in her large eyes. After I loaded my baggage, I stood on the train's steps at the last moment, and she said, "Will I see you in Baghdad, will I?" and I said, "Perhaps, perhaps . . . But my life is troubled, complicated. I might see you from a distance, from a distance only . . ."

I noticed that I had a copassenger in the car who was shyly observing the farewell scene through the glass. From his appearance and from the first word he uttered in English, thinking I was another foreigner, I knew that he was an Iraqi. The train moved, and the sad beautiful lady waved to me, and I waved to her, until each of us was no more to be seen by the other . . .

My cotraveler and I made acquaintance with each other in Arabic, and it turned out that he was returning from his studies in England and that we would board the same ship going from Marseilles to Beirut.

■ ■ ■

I did not spend much time in Beirut this time, because of my longing to return home to Bethlehem, where my mother and brothers were waiting for me. At noon, on the day after the ship dropped anchor in Beirut, I had lunch with my dear friends, Asim Salam and his wife Sulafa al-Khalidi, whom I had not seen since our many meetings in Jerusalem in 1945 and 1946. At four o'clock in the afternoon, I boarded the plane that took me to Qalandiya Airport, to the north of Jerusalem on the way to Ramallah. A meticulous search of arriving passengers' luggage took place at the airport following the assassination of the late King Abd Allah at the Aqsa Mosque in Jerusalem two or three weeks earlier. When I opened one of my suitcases, the many letters that I had received in Paris fell out, and the officer asked in surprise, "What is this?" I said, "Personal letters I've accumulated over a long time."

The officer collected the letters in a big heap, and it appeared he was going to confiscate them or seize them in order to read them in detail. But he changed his mind and took two or three letters from their envelopes, some in English, and he read what he could read. I was very embarrassed because he read the declarations of love, the mutual blame, and the petulant wrangling. However, he put the letters back in their envelopes, returned them to my suitcase and closed it, and saved me some embarrassment. (Ten years after that, I was returning from Beirut and, at the same airport, the customs' officer saw a copy of my translation of *Hamlet* in my suitcase and asked the very same question, "What is this?" I said, "A play by Shakespeare." He frowned and said, "Wait." He took the book to a special room to show it to his superior and tell him about the momentous thing he had come upon. A few minutes later, he returned, smiling, and said, "Please." He returned *Hamlet* to me safe and sound.)

■ ■ ■

"Lami^ca, Lami^ca!" said my brother Yousuf. "I notice that you keep repeating her name so many times."

His wife Thérèse said cunningly at the top of her voice, "What do you want from him? Leave him alone. He's free . . ."

Yousuf laughed as he put a record on the gramophone and said, "Her name is strange and beautiful. We'll see next summer what other strange and beautiful name you'll bring us from Baghdad!"

The tones of the first movement of Brahms's "First Symphony" sounded. Yousuf knew my fondness of Brahms's music in those days.

At that moment and as we were inundated with music, there was a knock on the outside door. I got up and opened the door and saw two beautiful young women. One of them was Sally Kassab, and we embraced warmly with joyful shouts. The other was a very shy young woman less than twenty years old and I welcomed her. Sally introduced her, Soraya Antonius.

Sally had married one of the high officers of the United Nations Refugees and Works Agency two or three years earlier. She lived in Jerusalem, and our friendship went back five years or more. It was one of those rare friendships that remain intimate, intellectual, and unblemished. Before the *nakba,* Sally visited me at my home in Jerusalem every two or three days, if we did not meet elsewhere. My mother liked her in a special way and preferred her to most of my other friends. I admired her personality and keen intelligence and followed her news with the attention of a friend who knew who loved her and whom she loved, and who in the end would win her. In the period when I moved in Jerusalem to live in the al-Qatamon neighborhood, our home became the meeting place for a circle of close friends, men and women, among whom Sally was the most prominent. Her coming to see me at our home in Bethlehem that afternoon after a long absence was a wonderful revival of Jerusalemite memories replete with emotions and associations. I called my mother and she came, and they both exchanged warm greetings and joy; then my mother withdrew to prepare coffee for us.

Two days earlier, I had accepted an invitation to lunch at the home of Mrs. Katie Antonius in East Jerusalem, and I found her as fully charming as I had always known her to be. She still sponsored Dar al-Awlad (Boys' Home) in Jerusalem with her own funds as I knew she had done for several years. In her large magnificent house, she still gave parties in which she always brought together men and women from among the Arabs and foreigners in Jerusalem, all of whom had important intellectual, social, or political positions. She was highly qualified for that activity not only because of her strong personality, attractiveness, and wealth but also because she was the widow of the famous thinker, George Antonius, whose fame increased after publishing in 1939 a book entitled *The Arab Awakening,* which was one of the most important books in English in those years, and later on, about the history of the Arab nationalist movement, including the Palestinian problem and its centrality among Arab causes. Among her other novel activities at one time was that now and then she organized parties known as moonlight parties in which she brought friends together on moonlit nights to spend an evening roaming on the walls of the old city of Jerusalem, which had been built by the Ottomans at the beginning of the sixteenth century.

Mrs. Katie Antonius said to me, "Soraya, my daughter, returned from England to spend the summer with us. Before she returns in a few days to continue her studies, I would like her to visit you so that you may tell her about existentialism. It seems that girls of her generation in England are taken with this fad, and she talks about it every day. Please, explain to her what this movement is all about, and rid me of it!"

When I met with Sally and Soraya in our sitting room, with Brahms still filling the air in a way my two visitors were not prepared for, it seemed to me that Soraya was moved in a manner I would not have expected. She sat by me on the inner sill of the double-arched window, by which Bethlehem's old houses with vaulted ceilings are distinguished. The room had the minimum furniture possible, and there were some of my paintings hung on the walls higgledy-piggledy and others leaning on ground-to-ceiling bookshelves stuffed with Arabic and English books in no order. The stone floor was covered only by a Bedouin rug of white-and-black goat hair, which reminded Sally that she had played with her puppy on it at one time in our home in al-Qatamon. Through the iron bars of the window, on whose outer sill stood pots of basil and geraniums, one could see the northern hills of Bethlehem stretching in the distance toward Jerusalem, and on the distant horizon stood the Convent of Saint Elias with its centuried steeple.

Of course, we did not talk about existentialism, for there were many other things of interest to talk about. I felt that Soraya had many questions and was very intelligent and quite articulate. It was very clear that she would soon become a writer one day—in English, though, because of her upbringing in England . . . And that is exactly what happened a few years later, after she took up residence in Beirut, and our friendship continued through the years and events. Perhaps the two Palestinian novels she published in London toward the end of the 1980s were, as she recently told me, mysteriously related to that beautiful afternoon visit she and Sally had surprised me with, which continued until just before nightfall.

■　■　■

On one of my evening walks with Yousuf in the direction of al-Madbasa, near the Young Men's Club, a radio was blaring songs and filling the air, when I heard a voice I recognized singing:

> We miss you, sweet one, by God we miss you,
> It's been a long time since you left us:
> The flame of distance is searing us
> And the fire of longing is burning us.
> We miss you, sweet one, by God we miss you . . .

I stood frozen in my tracks and suppressed a lump in my throat lest my groan be heard in the midst of that clamor. The song was one of Lamiᶜa's favorites, which she sometimes sang, and both of us liked the songstress and her other songs.

At that moment, I felt that Lamiᶜa was sending a cry for help. I was shaken and felt that I had to return to her in the fastest way . . . Returning to Lamiᶜa was absolutely necessary and to be done as quickly as possible.

But Mrs. Hulwa Jaqaman, president of the Women's Union

in Bethlehem, had negotiated with me two days after my arrival about giving a lecture at the union, and I had accepted. I had therefore to honor my commitment, however fiercely my yearning to see Baghdad took possession of me.

I delivered the lecture in a hall attached to the Young Men's Club, which was used as a cinema in the evenings. It brought back to me memories of the first months of the *nakba* three years earlier or a little more. That hall had been the meeting place of the people where I was elected by a large crowd of raging refugees as a member of a committee that had to be formed in the sudden absence of central authority after the shameful departure of the government of the British Mandate on May 14, 1948.

The audience this time was also large but it was not raging. The strange thing was that the lecture was at eleven o'clock on a Sunday morning, an hour not usual for lectures in other places, unless they were universities.

The subject of the lecture? "Woman: as she is and as she can be." I mentioned to the audience that Napoleon said, "I conquered and vanquished the whole world—and was conquered and vanquished by Josephine."

(5)

The year 1951 was distinguished in my life by the fact that I met Lami^{c}a, a most wonderful woman who would later accompany every step of my existence, strengthening me with extraordinary courage in experiences lasting forty years or more, which were mostly very troubled and intensely exciting—mad swings of fortune that sometimes brought us nightmarish periods of oppression, harshness, and suffering, and sometimes periods of ease, luxury, and pleasure that we almost did not believe to be ours.

It is strange that the year 1951 was also distinguished by the arrival in Baghdad of my friend, Dr. Ali Kamal, a professor and a psychiatrist. He was an old friend of mine since the time we first met in Jerusalem in our youth fourteen years earlier, the summer of 1937. We met outside the examination hall in the break between two examinations for the Palestine Matriculation Certificate. Brief though it was, this meeting left a deep effect on both of us and led to an intimate friendship beginning the middle of the following year after his return from his first year of study at the American University of Beirut and my obtaining a diploma in education from the Arab College. I was preparing myself at the time to travel to England for higher studies, but fortunately fate delayed my travel by one year to September of 1939. This permitted our friendship to mature and become intellectually richer in a glowing way through our discussions and writings—a matter I have spoken about on various occasions in my other books.

We remained closely in touch with each other all through the following years, seizing opportunities between my travels and his to spend some time together in long conversations. We also exchanged letters constantly wherever we were. But this is another story of my life and his, and has many details.

Since the latter part of 1948, after I had started working in Baghdad and he had returned to London to work as a psychiatrist, I tried to persuade him to come to Iraq with his family. He had gotten married in London in 1947, while I continued to be unable to settle down in a situation that would help me to get married.

My attempts to persuade him finally succeeded when he met in London with Tahsin Qadri, chief protocol officer at the Iraqi royal palace at the time and a man of progressive thought and great influence. Ali Kamal informed him that he wanted to work in Baghdad. Iraqi institutions were always inclined to employ Arab intellectuals who were experienced and proficient, wherever they found them, although salaries were not high. The crucial point in hiring them was the applicants' enthusiasm for the position. Among Palestinians, there had been an old partiality for Iraq that had increased since the middle of the 1930s because of their belief in the basic nationalist role which Iraq played in the life of the Arab world.

And this was what happened. Ali Kamal came to Iraq in that year, recommended by Tahsin Qadri, to work at the College of

Medicine in Baghdad with an annual contract similar to mine at the College of Arts; and he stayed in Baghdad all his life as I did and became one of the most famous physicians of Iraq and one of the foremost in scientific and cultural life. After my marriage, we remained—along with our two families—the closest of friends. Furthermore, in the 1960s, a few years after I had built my house on the street that is the twin of Princesses' Street in the Mansour Neighborhood, he insisted on living in our neighborhood and built himself a beautiful house near ours, on one of the streets branching off of Princesses' Street, the distance between our two homes being a few minutes' walk under the palms and eucalyptus trees.

■ ■ ■

Perhaps my return to Baghdad was a sort of confirmation that I had passed a turning point in my relationship with Lami^ca. After Paris and its excitements, I returned to Lami^ca to see her, as I had imagined her, actually glowing with cheerfulness and intelligence in every gesture, being distinguished in every limb of her body, and wearing dresses and gowns that set her apart from all the other women.

Our circle came back together and enlarged, and our meetings increased but the two of us did not neglect meeting alone whenever we could meet, mostly at Lami^ca's home, where we greeted the "lovers' plant" and offered it more tears and sighs. Among those added to our group, beginning in the autumn of that year, was Husayn Haddawi, who had just returned with his beautiful German wife, Krista, and rented a small house on the approaches of the Iron Bridge, branching off of the beginning of Imam al-Azam Street.

Buland al-Haydari used to talk a lot about his friend Husayn Haddawi, who had gone on a scholarship a few years earlier to the University of Nevada at Las Vegas to study English literature. When Husayn returned from his studies, the first of his close friends he saw was Buland. Buland introduced me to him in the early days after his arrival, and we discovered that he and I had both specialized in the same subject, with emphasis on modern writers like James Joyce, Eliot, and Virginia Wolf. A friendship soon arose between us, and it developed into an intimate bond that united a group that later became our own special circle. Our meetings at the home of Husayn and his wife often included Hilmi Samara, Evelyn, Ali Kamal and his wife Jane, Jawad Salim and his wife Lorna, Buland, Nizar Salim, and others including Lamiᶜa and me. Whenever Nizar came, he used to take out his large sketch-book and occupy himself with drawing caricatures of us, one by one: he was right, here, wrong, there; exaggerating one person's features, rendering another ugly—as his pen and his whimsical, jocular temperament led him.

At the beginning of the new academic year, a young woman with incredibly rosy cheeks attracted my attention and that of my colleague Desmond Stewart in the Department of English Literature at the College of Arts. She had two braids of thick, black hair that she tied behind her head to accentuate her long neck. Whenever she was addressed, because of her shyness, the rosy color of her cheeks turned into a wonderful red that contrasted with her white complexion that was not common among our students.

My colleague and I agreed on admitting this student without hesitation because of her obvious intelligence and quick wit even in English conversation. The name of this student, who distinguished herself among her classmates that year, was Balqis Sharara. Lamiᶜa later got acquainted with her through me, at one of the students' parties. Lamiᶜa and I did not know then—when our marriage was no more than an obscure, almost impossible desire of ours—that this attractive young woman would get married after a short period to Rifat al-Jadirji upon his return from his study of architecture in England and that a friendship would arise between our families and strengthen our deep intellectual bonds that would play a large part in our later life and would become stronger in time with their simultaneous cultural and social correlations.

■   ■   ■

As for my faithful female student, she continued to be faithful even after she became sure of my relationship with Lamiᶜa. I could not persuade her or myself that between the two of them

I was falling into a complex web considered to be illogical and irrational in our societal circumstances of those days. I later discovered that, whenever I wrote a short story, most of what I wrote related to my experiences preceding my arrival in Baghdad, for they had become whole and complete experiences with definite beginnings and definite ends. As for my experiences in Baghdad, their expression came to me in the form of poems that I was almost afraid to explain to myself or of paintings most of which I painted in a manner whereby I liberated myself psychologically by using symbols whose meanings I was only barely aware of. It was as if I was constructing puzzles for myself, the answers of which I feared or had no need for. All those paintings revolved either around Lami^ca or my faithful female student; and there was a certain face, perhaps mine, that was repeated in the middle or in the margins of the paintings, a haunted lost face on the edge of an indefinable sorrow.

One morning, I took a number of these oil paintings, mostly painted on paper (unfortunately, because many of them were destroyed or torn in later years), and I showed them to my female students in one of the poetry classes. One painting stood out, and the students stared at it persistently and engaged me in questions. My faithful student recognized that she was the one depicted in that surrealistic painting in which I merged her with the rocks and the sea as she held an open book in her hands. In the painting, there was an empty boat waiting on an abandoned shore; in the lower corner, there was a Palestinian hill with green olive trees and there was the same haunted face, or part of it, expressive of an invitation; there was also a beckoning hand, symbolic of escape, stretched out; on the margin, there was the face of another woman, a Byzantine face within a frame, an icon of pain, the meaning of which my faithful student immediately understood. That year, I had begun to teach these students Shakespeare's play *Twelfth Night* in which Viola disguised as a young man was in love with her master Duke Orsino, who, in turn, was in love with Olivia. Thinking that Viola was a youth, the duke often sent her as a messenger between himself and

Olivia, but Viola loved him and did not know how to express her love for him except by indirect means and by allusion, as sorrow ate at her heart like a worm . . . Shakespeare would in the end find a way out of this dilemma and please everyone, but we would remain in our dilemma, from which there was no escape except by denying it or running away from it.

At this time, I returned to a short story that I had begun to write while I lived in al-Qatamon in Jerusalem in 1947, which the events of the *nakba* had prevented me from completing. Its title was "The Meeting Place of Dreams." In fact, I had finished writing most of it at that time, and no more than a few pages remained. I knew exactly—in my mind—how to end the story, but for one reason or another, I had not written it, especially after being occupied in Baghdad by a long story entitled "The Floods and the Phoenix" that contained three sections, the last of which, entitled "Books and Two Handfuls of Dust," I had begun to write at that time.

I returned to "The Meeting Place of Dreams" and found that the prose I had achieved in it differed much in its language and internal consciousness from the prose of stories that I had read that year. In one of my translation classes, for which I chose paragraphs from contemporary Arab writings, it occurred to me to give my female students a paragraph from my story without mentioning that it was my own composition, and thus I would test their reaction, as well as their ability to translate it into English.

I began to dictate to my students the lines in which I described a rising evening storm, when the hero was in his secluded home far from the city. I reached the words in the text that said, "and a dazzling lightning flashed." No sooner had I uttered it, than I was surprised to hear the girls giggle and repeat after me, asking, "What flashed, sir?" I repeated, "and a dazzling lightning flashed." But they asked again, "Lightning flashed, sir?" and they laughed and enjoyed what they heard and wrote. One of the girls, my faithful student, said with sly cunning, "Do you hear? . . . 'a dazzling lightning flashed.'" All of a sudden, I understood that they intended something that had not occurred to me, innocent man that I was;

for by alluding to the literal meaning of her name, they clearly were referring to Lamiᶜa Barqi al-Askari,* my wonderful student's rival. They continued to emphasize the implications of the situation, and one girl said, "Also, 'dazzling,' sir?"

I then shouted at them, "Stop being silly! And let me continue . . ."

And I followed that with the next sentence and the one after it very quickly. But I found that it was difficult to ask them to translate what I had dictated, so I said, "I believe that this paragraph is difficult . . . Let's forget it. Here is another passage . . ."

It was clear that my faithful student knew everything about me and Lamiᶜa. She appeared to be yielding to the reality of my relationship with a woman whom she knew to be her rival, and who, she realized, was a professor and had a unique personality and enjoyed a freedom impossible for her as a student, unless it would be to show platonic love without end, a love that clung to her heart fiercely because it was never to be fulfilled.

(6)

Since my first hours in Baghdad, one of the most beautiful things I observed was the bond of friendship between young poets and writers and artists, who were resolute in advancing the revolution in techniques of writing and in styles of painting and sculpture. Traditionalists in writing and art naturally expressed their exasperation at these rebels, whom they accused of many things, both political and nonpolitical.

Buland al-Haydari, along with Adnan Raouf, Nizar Salim, and their friends, had established the Group of Lost Time three or four years earlier and started publishing a magazine. They also opened a small café on Antar Square at the entrance of al-Azamiyya, and they called it Waq al-Waq Café, but the police later closed it, fearing it was one of the nests of the leftist movements in those days, although not one of its owners or patrons was ever arrested. No more than twenty-six years old in 1951, Buland was representa-

---

*In Arabic, Lamiᶜa means flashing and Barq means lightning. *(Translator's note.)*

tive of the innovative writers in Baghdad and Jawad Salim at the age of thirty-two was representative of the artists. Their friendship was deep and of long standing. Some members of this group often had both literary and artistic aspirations, as was clear in the case of Nizar Salim, who wrote short stories in addition to painting and who was a few years younger than his brother Jawad. Another example is Shakir Hasan who "illustrated" his paintings with exquisite prose that was closer to poetry than to prose, and he also ventured into critical writing, theorizing for the Baghdad Modern Art Group as I used to do.

It was not difficult for me to see that the current of innovation in Iraq acquired much of its impulse and strength from this solidarity among writers and artists, which was not known to be as prominent among writers and artists in other Arab countries at that time. I found myself immersed in this great sea of innovation because my own biggest concern was simultaneously the word and the picture. Ever since I had returned to Jerusalem from my studies at Cambridge and ever since I had come to Baghdad from Jerusalem, I was filled with enthusiasm for ideas I had for new styles to be used by the Arabs in expressing themselves, this being an important means to renew the Arab self and excite its huge potential in a time of catastrophe.*

Since the exhibit of the Baghdad Modern Art Group in the spring of that year, Jawad, Buland, and I talked a lot about the necessity of gathering artists in an association; their numbers continually increased as they returned from studies abroad or graduated from the Institute of Fine Arts in Baghdad. We thought an association would organize them and not let them remain loosely associated "groups" with no ties except an agreement to put on an exhibit once every year or two, as the Pioneers had done under the leadership of Faiq Hasan. The previous year, the Pioneers had organized their first exhibit at the home of Dr. Khalid al-Qassab, who was an important painter although professionally he was a physician; and it was a truly pioneering exhibit as far as its size

---

*I spoke at some length about this matter in my book *al-Iktishaf wa al-Dahsha* (Discovery and Wonder).

and variety were concerned. But Jawad Salim, who had exhibited with them, was unhappy with it and felt he would not be satisfied with an exhibit in which there would not at least be a weak connecting thread or a common basic idea or a theoretical point of view that would be clear in the works exhibited. The result was that the Baghdad Modern Art Group put on its own exhibit, and some of its members had actually separated from the Pioneers, and joined Jawad and his friends and students.

Buland thought of persuading Jawad to seek the aid of an old friend of his, with whom he had a family relationship going back to the 1940s and who was the son of a leading politician who had gained the position of prime minister more than once. His friend's name was Nizar Ali Jawdat, and he had recently returned from the United States, where he had studied architecture. A year earlier, Jawad had put on his first one-man exhibit in his home, and it was there that I made Nizar's acquaintance. He had participated, although minimally, in the recent exhibit of the Baghdad Modern Art Group, and so we suspected that he must be strongly sympathetic to artists and could persuade his father to sponsor the project of an association for artists to be reestablished in Baghdad, ten years after the demise of the Friends of Art Association. Nizar's friend Khaldun Sati al-Husri was another old friend of Jawad's and his age and interested in the arts since the days of his studies at the American University of Beirut in the late 1930s and the early 1940s.

Eventually Jawad, Buland, and I agreed that we should visit Khaldun at his home one evening, and Khaldun informed Jawad that Nizar would be there with him. When we arrived at Khaldun's home, his wife asked us to wait because he had gone out earlier, promising to be back soon to receive us. Shortly afterwards, he came in with Nizar, who seemed to be in a state of extreme joy, and he and I renewed our acquaintance. Neither Jawad nor Buland wasted any time and immediately raised the subject of the association, and I supported them. Khaldun did not hesitate to commend the idea, and he too hoped that Nizar would persuade his father to embrace the idea and help it come together in a practical and official fashion.

However, Nizar began to mock the idea in a manner that surprised me, and he said, "What art? What artists? . . . These impostors make fun of your minds. They are a group of ignoramuses and profit-seekers . . . Leave them alone, my friends, and look for a way to occupy your time with something in which there is some real good . . . Do you know where we have just been, and why we have been late? We have been at the Semiramis Hotel at a reception for Rita Hayworth (she was at the height of her fame and charm in those days). A two-minute dance with Rita Hayworth is worth all your projects . . . Give us Rita Hayworth and forget associations, artists, and all this nonsense."

I was angry at his behavior and his words, and I realized that it was foolish to seek help from him for anything. I knew that Rita Hayworth was not in Baghdad and that he raved about her because he was intent on showing his indifference. I rose to my feet and said to Jawad and Buland, "Let's go!" and I moved toward the door. We left the two old friends in haste. On our way back, we agreed that an association for artists could only be established by the efforts of the artists themselves and their own organizing activities. And that was exactly what we worked toward in the following years until our ambition was realized in 1956.

However, it must be said that later a friendship grew between Khaldun, who became an important historian of modern Iraq, and me. I also became friends with Nizar Ali Jawdat after I met his American wife Elaine, an accomplished architect, when I found in both of them a serious interest in the modern architectural movement in Baghdad and noted their real contributions to its development. He and I often joked about his mocking manner that evening, which he, as I, had never forgotten, as it turned out.

■　■　■

My friendship with Ali Haydar al-Rikabi had remained warm since we had become acquainted in the last part of 1948. That was when I went to him, along with Desmond Stewart, who had recently arrived in Baghdad to teach, and we both offered to participate in the English language radio programs, for which he was then responsible in addition to his work at the royal court. Our programs were about the Palestinian cause, which was arousing a lot of enthusiasm and political debate. Later when my knowledge of cultural life in Baghdad grew, I also began to give radio talks about Arab poets and artists, the young Iraqis among them in particular. Although my writing for the radio was interrupted from time to time, the personal relationship Ali Haydar al-Rikabi and I had was never interrupted. At this time, I introduced Buland to him, and a friendship grew between them and continued for several years, during which Buland worked with Ali Haydar, by his arrangement, as his assistant in the administration of the al-Mansour Real Estate Company.

Also in 1948 I committed to Ali Haydar to offer a radio talk in English at regular intervals—as usual without remuneration—in which I would provide a commentary on the art movement in addition to my talks on the lively, literary movement. I had ascertained the importance of the modern poets and short-story writers in Baghdad and expressed my belief in the importance of the attempts of Nazik al-Malaika, whom I had become acquainted with through my student Mayy Samara, Hilmi's sister. Nazik wrote free verse and also daring theory to support it that I was among the first to uphold.

Ali Haydar al-Rikabi was several years older than any of us. He was the son of Rida Pasha al-Rikabi, who was of Syrian origin and had once been one of King Faysal's aides and the first prime minister of the emirate of Transjordan, established by Emir Abd Allah. Ali Haydar was distinguished by his broad learning and love of poetry, for he was a graduate of Victoria College in Alexandria, and he was distinguished also by his striking elegance in dress and lifestyle. He was a veteran of the Iraqi diplomatic corps, which in the 1940s and 1950s consisted of a number of the most eminent and cultured personalities that any advanced country could boast of regarding intelligence, experience, and patriotism. His wife, Mrs. Rabah, was a distinguished model of self-confidence, self-expression, and beautiful presence—qualities that Jawad Salim captured in the wonderful large painting he made of her, two or three years after those days of ours.

The dinner parties that Ali Haydar gave were highly regarded by us because he also invited the members of our circle to them. Lami^{c}a accompanied me sometimes, and among the guests were Buland, Desmond Stewart, and one or two other English professors with a modernist outlook who shared our interest in Arab causes and wrote on them. However, the most prominent remained Desmond Stewart, who dedicated his second novel on Iraq to Ali Haydar al-Rikabi.

That year Rosemary Boxer joined us. She was delicate and slim, and she loved debates. She had just arrived from Oxford and became one of my colleagues teaching English literature at Queen Aliya College. Her love for the Arab world started then, and circumstances soon helped her to become a permanent part of it.

■　■　■

At a short distance from the apartment where I lived, in the proximity of the Brazilian Café on al-Rashid Street, a vendor from northern Iraq used to set up a booth to sell olives in the evenings. I bought a kilogram of black olives from him, which I liked and which the people of the villages around Mosul pickled famously well. Heading for my apartment on foot, I ran into Lami^{c}a, accompanied by her friend Aliya al-Umari, whom I was very happy to meet and said to her, "Finally, at long last, you have become embodied! I thought that Lami^{c}a had invented you to instill in me a delusion that you existed."

She said, "But I have never thought that I would meet you with a bag of olives in your hand instead of a book of poetry!"

Lami^{c}a laughed and said, "Olives for him are no less important than poetry, for he comes from the land of olives."

Aliya interrupted, "Like us, like us, the people of Mosul."

I opened the paper bag and offered them its contents, but before they could apologize and decline, I said, "One olive at least for each of us, to be eaten as a communal ritual!"

"A beautiful idea!" exclaimed Aliya.

Each of them took an olive, glistening with oil, and I followed suit; and we ate our olives on the roadside.

Aliya suddenly asked, "When will you visit us?"

"When Lami^{c}a decides, " I said.

"Tomorrow," Lami‘a said, "Tomorrow evening, we'll come to your home together."

"Tomorrow evening, then," said Aliya, adding, "I can hardly believe it!"

I said, "It is the blessing of the olives . . ."

That was the beginning of a friendship or rather friendships that were among the best blessings that God granted us, Lami‘a and me, in the forty years we lived together.

■ ■ ■

When Lami‘a took me to Aliya's home in al-Aywadiyya near Bab al-Muazzam, I knew nothing about her husband, the architect Hazim Namiq except his name. Likewise, I knew nothing about the members of her family except a few names that came up in local newspapers because of their positions in the government and in society. However, Dr. Isam al-Umari, a recent graduate of the College of Medicine in Baghdad, was a member of our circle, especially latterly, and we met many times in the evening. I learned that Mrs. Suad, whom I had met before the summer holidays at the exhibit of Queen Aliya College and whose personality I admired, was his elder sister.

When Hazim and Aliya received us, I found that their home was simple and not distinguished in architectural style from most of Baghdad's homes built in the 1930s and 1940s in the neighborhoods branching off of al-Imam al-Azam Street. They were functional homes, economical in their building styles and room sizes. Their entrances were all of the same pattern, and many of their front doors still had a bronze knocker in the shape of a dove, to be used if the door bell did not work because the electricity was cut off.

I soon learned that Hazim, who had graduated in the middle of the 1930s from the University of Wales in Britain, was director general of the Department of Public Works in Iraq (in the early 1960s he would become the first president of the Iraqi Architects Association upon its establishment); I also learned that his elder brother Salim Namiq was a member of the House of Notables and a prominent farmer in Mosul. Both brothers were well educated, had wide knowledge, and liked collecting books. Two young men were staying at Hazim Namiq's home: Usama, Salim Namiq's son, who had recently returned from America where he studied mechanical engineering, and Hasan al-Umari, who was a student at the College of Law, whose father was the mayor of Mosul for many years, and who was Hazim's nephew and Aliya's cousin. Both young men were lively and merry in their continuous participation in our discussions and were interested in everything. The affection that grew between us all was immediate and continued to grow as days went by.

It was inevitable that I would meet soon with Mumtaz al-Umari, Aliya's elder brother, who was in his middle thirties and director general of the Ministry of the Interior. He was a man of strong presence wherever he went, for he was dignified and serious and both loved and feared by members of his family, who had a great deal of respect for his opinion, exactly as they did with the opinion of his wife and cousin Suad. As for his younger brother Nathir and his wife Mayy al-Umari, I heard a lot about them but did not meet them because they were in Beirut where Nathir worked at the Iraqi embassy. I also heard a lot about Imad, Isam's younger brother, who also worked in the diplomatic corps abroad.

My relationship with them all would become strong through Lamiᶜa because she had a special central position among them on account of her and her mother's connections with the family since the time they were all in Mosul in the early 1930s and thereafter. Lamiᶜa was the only one who was not from the al-Umari family (whose roots went back to Caliph Umar ibn al-Khattab), but she was the closest person to them in all matters of her life and theirs.

Lamiᶜa and I continued to meet in the evenings with our circle of friends at the home of Qahtan Awni or Husayn Haddawi; or the two of us met alone mostly at Lamiᶜa's home, either in her mother's presence or without it. But now we began to meet also at family gatherings almost every evening at Hazim and Aliya's home because Hazim was not inclined to go out at night to visit anyone, even his relatives. He made it a rule for members of his large family and their close friends to meet at his home every evening, where everyone was offered drinks and food with enormous generosity.

All this of course did not distract me from my heavy work at the College of Arts and at Queen Aliya College, but I gave up my lecturing at the Higher Teachers' College in order to give more time to my lectures at Queen Aliya College. This I did in compliance with the desire of Mrs. Sarah al-Jamali, who was the head of the Department of English Literature and who made me responsible for developing new syllabi and deciding on higher-level textbooks to be taught in her department. She was an exemplary lady in her assiduous devotion to work and her eagerness for its details. In addition to her teaching duties, she continually organized activities and important social services, which would have weighed heavily even upon specialists. She was the wife of Dr. Muhammad Fadil al-Jamali, who was a minister several times and would later be prime minister more than once.

When did I write, then? When did I paint? When did I read? I don't know. But I wrote a lot, painted a lot, and read a lot in that busy atmosphere, which Lami‘a filled with radiance and vitality. Perhaps my day was more than twenty-four hours, and that I should sleep sometimes did not occur to me until I fell unconscious on my bed and sank immediately into a dark daze to find that a new wonderful day was rising and that Athena, my housekeeper, had prepared a magnificent breakfast for me.

Whenever I took the bus from my apartment to college or to meet Lami‘a, I made sure that I had a book in my pocket to pull out and read during the slow movement of the bus along al-Rashid Street or al-Imam al-Azam Street. On those trips to and fro, I read many books, some of which required concentration and close attention that were not easily afforded by the passengers getting on and off the bus, when it stopped every two hundred meters or less.

(7)

From time to time, Khalid al-Rahhal (one of the members of the Baghdad Modern Art Group), used to pay me a surprise visit that was as sweeping as a hurricane. He would inform me of his latest sculpture, the last person he had fallen in love with, or the last person with whom he had quarreled at the Institute of Fine Arts, where he taught sculpture along with Jawad Salim. Like most artists, he was an extreme egotist and so self-centered that he was not interested in talking about anything but himself and his own concerns, and he could not listen to anything about anybody else or about any subject unrelated to what he was involved in.

He was interested in letting me know about any new thing he made, as had been so since I made his acquaintance early in 1949, when he took me to al-Khudayri's palace in al-Jadiriyya to see the sculpture he had done in stone for the house's owner in the middle 1940s. He was only in his early twenties and moti-vated by an astonishing talent nourished by no real knowledge but what he saw with his own eyes and touched with his own hands and his long contemplation of the Assyrian sculpture in the Iraqi museum that had had a deep influence on his style and vision until the end of his life. The other influence on his vision was, as he told me, what he was taught by the sculptress Heidi Lloyd, wife of the archaeologist Seton Lloyd, during the period he was her student at the Institute of Fine Arts.

What I also admired in him in those days was his ability to make line drawings in ink of the figures of women and oxen that blended tenderness, strength, and an easy flow, the likes of which only great artists are capable of.

My astonishment at his talent was augmented when he invited me one day to his home in an old, miserable building in al-Fadl neighborhood near al-Maydan. It was a small room, whose floor was covered by straw mats; it had one chair and a little, worn table; it also had a box, which was really a box of wonders, for when he opened it, he pulled out of it one line drawing in ink after another for my eyes to feast on; they were some of the most beautiful things I have ever seen, and he gave me a number of those drawings that had accumulated.

He constantly seemed to be excited. He spoke with the least logic and coherence possible, using as many surrealistic expressions and images as possible. Without intending it, his words suggested a sense of humor that made the listener laugh, while simultaneously keeping him sympathetic for the artist's enthusiasm.

His relief sculpture, representing women in a public bath, executed in the style of a relief discovered in Ashurbanipal's palace in Nineveh, is one of the most wonderful of his sculptures in those days. Despite the many beautiful sculptures he did later, he did not achieve another that exceeded the spontaneity of this relief and its distinctive Iraqi vision that was all his own.

One day in 1949, he was in my room at Preparatory College in al-Azamiyya where I lived, and he was showing me statuettes he had carved. Some of them were of ivory and some of marble. He pulled them out of his handbag like a magician pulling rabbits out of his hat. What a set of beautiful, expressive, surprising statuettes they were, representing the forms of women belonging to the circle of the Babylonian god, Abo, and his female companions standing by and beseeching unknown powers: very modern, yet as ancient as history!

With me in the room that day was my colleague, Fahd al-Rimawi, a Palestinian who had graduated from the College of Arts in Cairo. He belonged to a religio-political movement calling on Arabs to reject modern civilization and return to the desert, which they perceived as the original source of their power. As I was discussing the artistic qualities of these carvings with Khalid, Fahd contemplated them and smiled with wonderment. Then he said, "Your art is very strange, man. Pure Arabs reject art, especially sculpture. Yet, you never cease sculpting."

In all innocence, Khalid answered, "But my mother is Armenian."

Fahd laughed, feeling he had put his finger on the secret, and exclaimed, "Now I know from where this crazy aberration has come to you."

(Fahd was admired by our other colleague, Desmond Stewart, who based the protagonist in his first novel, *Leopard in the Grass* on him, as I did a short while later in my portrayal of one of the important characters of my novel, *Hunters in a Narrow Street.*)

From that moment, I made an effort to persuade Dr. Matta Aqrawi, director general of higher education, to send that natively talented young man, Khalid al-Rahhal, on scholarship to Italy. Dr. Aqrawi said he wished he could do that but added that Khalid had not finished his secondary school education and appeared to be unable to do so. Dr. Aqrawi wondered how Khalid could ever be selected for a scholarship. I said, "Beethoven was unable to learn the multiplication tables all his life . . . Khalid is not in need of physics and mathematics. He thinks with his hands, only with his hands, when they work with stone and the chisel."

My efforts were successful in the end, and Khalid was sent to Rome at the beginning of 1954 with a special fellowship in accordance with a cultural agreement made with the Italian embassy that was not subject to the usual conditions of scholarships of the Iraqi Ministry of Education. I met him with other artists when I passed through Rome for a few days on my way back to Baghdad from Harvard in the spring of that year.

I had another artist friend, who visited me often and who was not in the least like Khalid or any other person. His name was Munir-Allah Wardi, and he was a mechanical engineer who had studied abroad. His hobby, however, overshadowed his profession, for he played the clarinet so skillfully that he became the principal player of the wind instruments of the Iraqi Symphony Orchestra, which had been reestablished toward the end of the 1940s. Munir was a friend and colleague of my friend Hilmi Samara at the College of Engineering, and our conversations on music, when we met, were interspersed only by conversations on mathematics.

Munir agreed to give me lessons in solfège and harmony once a week. He came to my apartment, carrying the sheet music, and I would follow with him in my music lessons. I was very happy that he always expressed his astonishment at my continued progress. However, he complained—as I did—about the lack of a piano in my apartment to help clarify theoretical details. One day, he said, jokingly, "I have nothing more to teach you musically but to play the clarinet!"

The other musician who equaled him in generosity of spirit and love for musical compositions was Fuad Rida, first viola in the Iraqi Symphony Orchestra. My long friendship with him started early in 1949 when I discovered our common love for classical music. Since I did not have my own phonograph and records, he regularly came to my apartment carrying his phonograph and different records every time. In the beginning, we listened to the works of Gabriel Fauré, whose *Requiem* we listened to again and again, and analyzed again and again, along with the *Pavane* and other compositions of his.

One day he came to me with César Franck's wonderful sonata for violin and piano. This sonata always reminded me of when I first immersed myself in classical music, in 1938 when I was a student at the Arab College in Jerusalem. I was the student responsible for the library and also for the music collection that had come to us as a gift, with a large elegant phonograph, from the British High Commissioner, Sir Arthur Wauchope, whose magnificent residence stood a short distance from our college on Mount al-Mukabbir. I used to seek privacy in the large hall to play this sonata, which suggested wonderful visions of love to me, as we lived like monks in the college. It made me imagine seeing our neighbor Anahid from the window. She was two years younger than I, and I saw her settled among the branches of a large rose bush, swinging one leg; whenever she touched the branches with her bare foot, rose petals fell on her then to the ground. (She used to wait for my return home from college every Friday morning; and as soon as I arrived, I played a special tune for her on my accordion, and she responded from her home, overlooking the courtyard of our home, by playing a special tune on her piano.)

When I finished listening to César Franck's sonata, I played the records of *Scheherazade* by Rimski-Korsakov, and they were no less exciting to my frantic artistic imaginings and took me across Sindbadian seas; or I moved to Beethoven's sixth symphony, the *Pastoral,* to fill the forests of the world with screams and songs . . .

Such were the beginnings of my obsession with music, which later accompanied me to England and grew stronger there and in the period that followed in our home in Jerusalem with my brother Yousuf and at the Arts Club at the Jerusalem YMCA.

(8)

When I first established a Classical Music Association for my students, they contributed small amounts of money, which one of them collected and with which, after consulting me, he bought the records available in Baghdad for us to play on musical evenings. I introduced each piece by explaining as best I could why this music should excite these enthusiastic students' imaginations, and I hoped that I could lead to some love for what they listened to and to an understanding of a concept other than *tarab* (rapturous delight), to which they were accustomed in Arab music. I also emphasized this art's connections to the other arts and literature that they studied.

At the beginning of the academic year in the fall of 1951, I was surprised at the growth of the number of listeners and at the fact that many professors joined, in addition to the students' friends and professors from other colleges. The dean, Dr. Abd al-Aziz al-Douri, was enthusiastic about these evenings and made sure they became social events in which tea with milk was offered and sometimes cakes. He then secured an important source for many more records and a phonograph with large loudspeakers, borrowed from the library of the British Council. I don't deny that I, being a lover of music in a country where classical records were rare, benefited a lot from my responsibility to the growing audience; for I had to prepare myself for every musical evening by referring to books that would help me in giving information about every musical work that I introduced.

What wonderful enthusiasm that was on the part of all those people who had become accustomed to meeting with us every week or two in the College of Arts hall, from the dean and professors, to the male and female students, and finally our Iraqi and foreign friends. When we noticed that a good number of professors of other nationalities, especially English, were in the audience, I started to add a few words in English to my Arabic introduction. Speaking about western music in English is naturally easier and more accurate than in Arabic. Some members of my and Lami^{c}a's circle were usually present in the audience.

At a certain point toward the end of that year or the beginning of the next, I noticed that my colleague, Dr. Salih Ahmad al-Ali, came to our musical evenings with an English friend of his. He soon introduced me and my friend Hilmi Samara as well, for they both had been students at Oxford University as recently as a year earlier or a little more, and when they finished their studies, Dr. Salih returned to Baghdad as a professor of Arab history while his friend, Frank Stokes, joined the Iraq Petroleum Company, which had brought him to Baghdad because of his fluent knowledge of Arabic in order to establish a department of public relations for the company. His acquaintance was the first contact that Hilmi and I had with this large company, which we knew played a prominent role in Iraq's political and economic life. It was about to sign an important agreement with the Iraqi government in which profits would be shared half-and-half for the first time in the history of Iraq or any other oil-producing country in the region. And people expected, whether they were satisfied with the agreement or not, that millions of dinars would suddenly flow to them, after a long period of economic difficulty. A development board, headed by a former minister, Arshad al-Umari, was established by the government so that the incoming funds would be spent in a manner that would lead to the country's progress; and the board started to make ambitious plans, in consultation with Iraqi and foreign experts, for wide development in a country whose population at the time did not exceed five million people.

In that period, the Ministry of Education was responsible for higher education (since the University of Baghdad had not yet been established, and the College of Arts and Sciences was still at the stage of being studied by experts before being declared a full-fledged university accredited abroad). We noticed that the Ministry of Education lost much of its earlier, very warm enthusiasm for the Palestinians it had made contracts with

136

following the *nakba* of 1948 when it appointed hundreds of Palestinians as teachers in elementary and secondary schools and as professors in the university colleges of Baghdad. Since the beginning of my third academic year, 1950–1951, the number of Palestinians whose contracts were renewed decreased greatly, and the decrease was continuing in an obvious manner at the beginning of the following academic year. In the summer, the contracts of many of those professors were terminated, and some of our colleagues were among them. This made Hilmi and me, as well as others, realize that the summer of 1952 would see the end of all our contracts. We had therefore to consider our situation and think of alternatives, although Hilmi and I continued to be fond of Iraq and to hope that the responsible officials, many of whom had become our friends, would find a way to avoid our positions being lost. Although one of my friends, Professor Farid Hananiyya, whom I had met in Bethlehem at the end of the previous summer, suggested that I should join the teaching staff of the American University of Beirut, where he worked as dean of the humanities, I was not much excited at that prospect because Lamiᶜa beckoned to me from a distance to return to her and I had become some small part of the cultural life in Baghdad and its huge future potential, to which I had become thoroughly committed.

In that period, I brought my younger brother Isa from Bethlehem to live with me, and he found a job in a firm specializing in imports and exports, the owners of which were Palestinian and with whom it pleased him to work.

One morning, as I was talking with Albertine Juwaida, one of the history professors at Queen Aliya College, she sought my advice regarding the wording of a paragraph in a letter she had written in English that she was sending to the Rockefeller Foundation in New York. When I asked her for more information about this famous foundation, she said that it had recently granted research fellowships to a number of professors in Baghdad and that she was now negotiating with one of its officials about a fellowship to assist her in obtaining a doctorate. The name of that official was John Marshall.

I asked her hesitatingly, "If I write to him, do you think he will be interested in answering me?"

She said, "Certainly. With your academic background and writings, and with your competence in English, you will find no difficulty in persuading a man like John Marshall of what you want. What do you want exactly?"

I said, "I don't know. I would like to return to an atmosphere like the one I knew at Cambridge University and stay in it for a year or two."

A thought flashed in my mind at that moment, as though falling from heaven: I should do research at Cambridge, so long as my future in Baghdad was not secure for more than a few more months. After my research and study, who knew where I would be?

I got the foundation's address from Albertine and wrote a letter to John Marshall two or three days later. In it I gave him some details of my curriculum vitae and asked for the foundation's aid in spending a year or two at Cambridge to do research on literary criticism.

The only person I informed about the letter was, of course, Lami͑a, who, it turned out, was no less anxious about me than I was about myself with regard to what could happen after the current academic year; and the idea of the fellowship appealed to her.

In that context, we spoke for the first time about our desire to get married, whatever the difficulties. We spoke about marriage as inevitable after about one year of experiencing a love that made us see that life without it would be impossible for both of us. As for the difficulties, they were many and varied, and some of them seemed insurmountable, but we had to face them and transcend them. We continued to hope that if we got married and went abroad together to study for one year or two, we would return to Baghdad, and I would go back to teaching again at the College of Arts

Two or three weeks later, I received a telegram from John Marshall saying that he had received my letter and that he was coming soon to Baghdad for an educational task and would seek an interview with me upon his arrival in order to help him make a decision about my request.

In those months, Adnan Raouf worked at the Iraq Petroleum Company in the north but never missed an opportunity to come to Baghdad. So we met, not only with Buland and Nizar, but also with our special group of which he was one of the first members and which remained a beautiful blend of men and women among whom relationships had become clear, all indicating imminent marriages.

It so happened that Amer al-Askari, Lami^ca's elder and only brother, was on leave in Baghdad from his job as administrator of the subdistrict of Zammar in the district of Mosul. His friend Adnan arranged a meeting for me with him, and we went on a picnic to the gardens of al-Jadiriyya with two or three others. We enjoyed ourselves very much, combining the joy of conversation with the pleasure of eating chickens roasted on wood in the open air. Amer told me that he had heard a lot about me and that he read what writings of mine reached him in his remote location. I immediately liked him for his frankness, his open mind, and his constant good humor that contributed to an atmosphere of continuous merriment.

He later took more leaves in order to come to Baghdad, where I would see him with Lami^ca and Adnan. He was not interested in meeting our other friends because, as I noticed, he was overwhelmingly shy especially around women and because he had another group of close friends with whom we had no bonds of acquaintance or interest.

■ ■ ■

Among the beautiful coincidences of my life was that, from the time of my secondary studies in Jerusalem, many of my best friends were from the region of Tulkarm in Palestine despite its distance from Jerusalem. The first of them was Ahmad al-Hajj Abd al-Rahman; then I made the acquaintance of Ali Kamal and the poet Abd al-Rahim Mahmoud—all of whom were from Anabta in the district of Tulkarm. There were also others who were of significance in my life. After poet Ibrahim Touqan stopped teaching us when I was in my last year of elementary school at al-Rashidiyya School, I was taught Arabic there by Abd al-Karim al-Karmi, the famous poet known as Abou Salma; his brother, the great linguist and lexicographer Hasan al-Karmi, taught me English for three years at the Arab College; both brothers were among the notables of Tulkarm, and friendly relations continued among us for all the following years. Then there was Hilmi Samara, also from the district of Tulkarm.

I knew Hilmi as a student at the Arab College. He was two years younger than I and filled the corridors of the college with the clamor of his constant arguments with this student and that; for he had an extraordinary intelligence and was a genius in mathematics in particular. He and I were both sent to study in England in 1939. I went to the University of Exeter the first year and then to Cambridge later on. Hilmi first went to the University of Nottingham to study mathematics, and three years later he won the Lubbock Award granted to the student who ranks first in the bachelor's examinations in mathematics among all the students of Britain examined by the University of London.

He continued his studies at Nottingham and, two years later, won the highest grade in physics too. A year earlier, I had decided to return to Jerusalem, but Hilmi moved to the University of Cambridge, where he obtained a doctorate in quantum mechanics, a science combining mathematics and physics, and he returned to Jerusalem in the summer of 1947 as a professor at the Arab College, while I was a professor of English literature at al-Rashidiyya College.

A few months later, the events of the *nakba* carried us away, and the professors of both colleges were dispersed and found themselves scattered among the universities and colleges of the Arab world. And lo and behold, Hilmi and I met again in Baghdad in the fall of 1948 and once more shared a turbulent and exciting life. He was appointed a professor at the Higher Teachers' College and a lecturer at the College of Engineering and the College of Arts and Sciences.

If Baghdad in that period knew a genius in the sciences apart from Dr. Abd al-Jabbar Abdallah, it was no doubt this green-eyed young man hailing from a village in Palestine. His voice again resounded in the corridors of the colleges, whose students did not know a professor who equaled him in intelligence, knowledge, quick-wittedness, and capability to solve recondite problems of mathematics and physics.

Perhaps it is strange that the things we had in common between us—literature and art on the one hand and the mathematical and physical sciences on the other—were not necessarily great; but our responses to issues of thought and to life experience were similar in kind and strength. Our friendship remained deep throughout half a century and was never shaken by events or the vicissitudes of time, by wonderful developments as well as abominable ones.

■ ■ ■

In the spring months of 1952, events followed each other in close succession and they interacted in such a way as to make it seem as if fate was organizing and moving them in a purposeful way in order to create a destiny for me that I could only know as it developed part by part. Then, lo and behold, in time the parts became a complete whole that gave life, my life at least, a form that could be seen in the mind as the details of a Greek play would; and like a Greek play, its meaning reverberated endlessly.

John Marshall came to Baghdad and stayed at the Ziya Hotel, which was close to my apartment. He visited the deans' offices at the College of Arts and Queen Aliya College. A day or two later, he asked me to go and see him at the hotel in the evening. When I did, I found that he was so frank, friendly, and very warm that one could only reciprocate affectionately.

It seemed that, in the few days he spent in Baghdad before I visited him, he had sought information about me from more than one person and in more than one place, and I got the impression that he had already decided that his foundation would grant me "a research fellowship in literary criticism" for one year, which might be later extended by six months.

I could hardly believe what I heard him say. Without knowing it, he gave me a promise of a new life in which I would retain

141

my freedom for at least one more year, during which I would devote myself to reading and writing as I wished and would have in my company the woman without whom life for me would not have been possible.

However, he raised the issue of my going to Cambridge, to my own university in England, as I had requested. He said that he would prefer that I change my mind and go to Cambridge, Massachusetts, to Harvard University, from which he had graduated. "I know," he said trying to persuade me, "that you, the British Cambridge set, imagine that there is no other university in the world that can compare. That's fine. But come to Harvard and try our university. I am confident that you will not regret that."

After I hesitated, he reminded me that Harvard today was one of the world's greatest universities, so I accepted. I thought that by going to America, I would acquire direct knowledge of the United States, which I had not yet experienced and whose importance, as was clear in the middle of the twentieth century, would only increase in determining the future world's civilization before the end of the century. Furthermore, I thought that American literature, despite its roots in European literature, especially England's, now rivaled it in breadth of vision and in the depth of its probing of the human spirit. (When I told someone in Cambridge, Massachusetts, a year later that I was writing a long novel, thus suggesting my ambition was to produce a unique and important book, I will never forget that he laughed and said, "So what? You may not know that in every other house in this city at this moment, there is someone who is writing a new, important book—like you!")

Our meeting ended in the best manner but at the last moment Marshall said, "Of course, you will have to wait for my written approval. When I return to New York, I will get in touch with Harvard University concerning your admission there to do research in literary criticism, and when I am sure of everything, I will write to you in detail. Most probably, we will see you toward the end of September when the new academic year begins. Meanwhile, you have to make arrangements with the College of

Arts here and make sure it will keep your position for you on its teaching staff during your absence, however long it may be."

I answered in a way that I thought would reassure him that the matter was quite simple and guaranteed, but deep down I knew that it was not. I hoped that I would not have to wait too long for his reply.

Yet his reply did seem long in coming . . . perhaps because of the anxiety that beset me and gripped me in a manner I had not experienced for many years.

■　■　■

At that time, I completed writing "Love and Two Handfuls of Earth" and sent it to *al-Adib* magazine in Beirut for publication. The story was the third and last part of "The Floods and the Phoenix." The title that I had given the trilogy was, no doubt, an unconscious echo of my experience with Lami^ca during those months. I wanted to explore Solomon's saying in the Song of Songs, which the heroine of the trilogy quotes:

> " . . . for love is strong as death;
> . . . .
> Many waters cannot quench love,
> neither can the floods drown it."

As is suggested in the three stories, Sheila, the heroine, is only partially based on Gladys Newby, the most intelligent and beautiful young woman I knew and loved when I was a student in England, both of us graduating in 1943. Yet the floods did come later, and they were devastating and drowned that love.

After the passage of some years, I had to complete writing "The Floods and the Phoenix" to indicate the passing of one wonderful woman from my life finally and the entrance of another. Perhaps that was the reason why such a long period of time passed between my writing the first part of the trilogy and the last two, for I began them when Lami^ca took her place in the depths of my being and allowed me to experience a new love that entered frolicking, laughing, shining, on the heels of a love drowned by the floods.

It is strange that real floods had a symbolic effect on me and released me into the space of a new experience, of which I could not have conceived before. For in the night of the fifth of January 1948, the streets of Jerusalem flooded during violent thunderstorms that brought with them a heavy rain that lasted for many hours. The water flooded Jawrat al-Nisnas (below Mamilla Road) and burst into our home, which I had left in order to reside in al-Qatamon. The water rose inside the house, and the current carried out a big tin box full of Gladys's letters, among other things. It carried the box like a derelict boat to the nearby courtyard. The box then capsized in the turbulent motion of the torrential stream and its loose cover fell off. The letters were thrown out and scattered all over the surface of the large pool that formed between the rocks and tree trunks.

That very night, in the ill-starred hours after midnight, Jewish terrorists blew up the Semiramis Hotel near our home in al-Qatamon. The earth and its flood shook in the stark darkness. Many were killed and others injured in the explosion, among whom were several friends of mine. My brother Murad came to us early in the morning after having heard the news of the explosion on the radio. When he saw us alive—my mother, my brother Yousuf and his new bride, my brother Isa, and myself—despite the terror we had gone through that night, he started crying, out of a mixture of pain and joy. The two old, miserable rifles in the house had remained resting in a corner because they proved to be useless in confronting the murderers, who escaped under cover of darkness and the heavy rain. We had only to thank God for the well-being of those who were safe in the midst of that terrible tragedy . . .

Murad described for us the flood that had taken place at our former home, for he lived with his wife and three children in a nearby house, whose relative elevation helped it escape inundation except for a little part . . . He then spoke of the hundreds of papers and envelopes that lay scattered about the courtyard as the water receded when the rain stopped and the drains were unblocked by the people of the neighborhood. He knew only that those papers must have been important to me. Among the things

I did in the afternoon of that sorrowful and heart-rending day was to go with my brothers to Jawrat al-Nisnas, where we collected the scattered love letters, many of which were caught on the rocks and old tree trunks. Their ink had run, although some of them were still somewhat readable, but many were dyed the color of ink or their lines totally erased. Those that were folded were also drenched, and they disintegrated as soon as they were opened.

I was greatly surprised at that moment to see a scene come to life that I had described about two years earlier in my short novel *Screams in a Long Night*. It was as though I had prophesied that hellish night.

The floods and the phoenix . . . I believed in the phoenix. I believed in great renewal after every severe trial. I believed new beginnings rising once again from the ashes of the burning fire. Although in my trilogy I spoke about the phoenix in the context of the nation's renewal, I was speaking—consciously or unconsciously—about my own personal experience. I saw in every event or relationship that I experienced something of that fire from which I could arise through the flames and smoke like the legendary bird. I could not speak about such feelings in those days except obliquely and allusively, for I was sometimes afraid that my phoenix would disappoint me one day, but I would then say, "No, the phoenix will never disappoint me."

(9)

I had an appointment with Lami^{c}a for lunch at the Sindbad Hotel. But she telephoned the hotel, where I was waiting for her, and informed me that she had been detained by an emergency that would keep her occupied for the rest of the day. So I took my lunch alone, then went up to my room in the apartment and tried to have a short nap in my comfortable chair. When I could not sleep, I got up and went to my papers and oil paintings. I remembered my promise to paint my blue tableau, *The Woman Who Dreamt She Was the Sea,* which Lami^{c}a had demanded of me more than once. But I was preoccupied with another idea, the idea of this face—Lami^ca's—that appeared to me wherever I turned, and I had to actually see it in order to be able to think of anything else. In recent months, I had drawn in ink as well as in pencil more than one line drawing of Lami^ca, although she never stayed put on her seat more than two minutes without some sort of motion, conversation, or laughter. Her face filled my vision: the locks of her hair arranged in two crescents on either side of her forehead, her large black eyes, her nose that suggested self-assuredness and strength, her upper lip clearly defined like the bow of the god of love, her lower lip shaped like a half of a fruit that tempted one to bite it, her wine-colored dress with an open collar revealing her long neck and shoulders and collarbones, which I used to tell her that I wanted to write verses of poetry across in a magical language that no one but us knew . . .

I had no choice but to put a sheet of drawing paper on a board and paint with my brush and oil colors in order to compensate for her absence by creating her on paper.

In two hours or less, Lami^ca was before me, her head lowered a little, as it had been when she sat near the wide window at her home where she had once watered the lovers' plant daily, as we both did later, with tears and sighs.

I gazed with rapture at the exact resemblance of Lami^ca that I had painted, compelled by the power of memory . . . Then I went to the bathroom and washed my hands stained with the paints. Hearing Mrs. Athena's movement in the kitchen, I dropped in there and asked her to make me a cup of tea.

A few minutes later, she brought me the tea and noticed the painting that stood there. As I was taking the first sip from the cup, she said in her charming Greek accent, "Ah, Professor! Has Miss Lami^ca been here today in my absence?"

I said, "No, not at all." For whenever Lami^ca arranged to come to my apartment, I used to ask my hostess's permission, who then received Lami^ca herself upon her arrival and made tea or coffee for us. Athena had thought that I had "smuggled" my girlfriend to the apartment this time without her knowledge.

However, Athena insisted that Lami^ca had come and that I had not told her. When I denied it again, she said, "I made your room this morning, and I went in there again at noon to be sure I made it. Both times, the picture of Miss Lamiᶜa was not there. And here she is now in front of me." (She came closer to the painting and cautiously touched its wet surface with her finger.) "The oil has not even dried yet . . . She did come, and you painted her in my absence."

I then laughed heartily and said, "Oh, Madam Athena! My attempt has then succeeded! I have just painted this painting from memory . . ."

She took out her eyeglasses, put them on, and scrutinized the painting, saying, "I can't believe it, I can never believe it." She then went out, giving me a suspicious look, persistent in her belief that Lamiᶜa had been with me all afternoon that day.

If I had not feared she would misunderstand me, I would have said to her, "Of course she has been with me all afternoon today, and she will be with me tonight and tomorrow, in the morning, in the forenoon, and in the evening. And I shall not deny that if you ask me again about her . . ."

In the afternoon of the next day, as soon as I returned from college and had something to eat, I began to paint *The Woman Who Dreamt She Was the Sea* for the second time, in order to fulfill my promise. The woman emerged before me, creature of the waves and dreams, nibbled by the clouds as though by rapacious and predatory beasts, and abiding in the obscurity of the water and its eternal continuity.

■　■　■

What for months I had suspected would happen finally came true. Just before the year's final examinations or perhaps just after them, the dean of the College of Arts and Sciences asked me to meet with him privately. I had always entertained a deep respect for the dean, Dr. Abd al-Aziz al-Douri, for his prominent position as an Arab historian and for his administrative experience in running a college, the importance of which in the educational life of the country continued to increase. Furthermore, I never forgot that he was the man I had met one day in September of 1948 at the Iraqi embassy in Damascus and asked for a job in Baghdad.

Hardly had he seen me and read my papers, when he immediately completed the details of my appointment to teach in the colleges of Iraq and without hesitation made arrangements for me to travel to Iraq. That was the beginning of an affection between us and a gratefulness on my part that continued over the years, even after he left Iraq. Without either of us knowing it at the time, he was the decisive factor at the most important turning point of my life, for he was the one who decided that I should go to Baghdad, where my life was formed anew.

When I entered his office, he received me warmly, but anxiety was clearly visible on his face. As usual, he ordered a cup of tea for me; then he asked me questions of a general nature. It appeared that he wanted to broach a subject that was difficult for him. Finally he opened a file that was in front of him and said, "I don't know how I can break what is in this file to you, who have become an integral part of this college . . . I have received an order from the Council of Higher Education not to renew your contract, and I assure you that this order was made without my being consulted. You are not the only professor whose contract it was decided not to renew, but I wish this decision had not been made . . ."

At that moment, I remembered a meeting of the council of professors held more than a year earlier, which I had entered late for some reason. When I arrived, I found that the professors, looking for a motto for the college, had decided to adopt the Qur'anic verse that says, "And of knowledge, you have been given but a little." My immediate reaction was, "But there is another verse which, I feel, is the ideal motto for a college specializing in arts and sciences as our college; and it is the verse that says, 'And say: Lord, increase my knowledge.' What do you think?" I was pleased to see that the dean was excited by this motto, which in fact had been my personal one since my youth. The professors responded positively with no objection and decided to make this Qur'anic verse the motto of the college. I fully and inexplicably identified with this new educational entity, of which I was one of the founding professors. When Dr. Abd al-Aziz al-Douri decided in Damascus to appoint me as a professor, he informed me that the college in which I was going to teach was to become the nucleus of the University of Baghdad, which was then in the phase of planning; and it was a cause of joy for me on that day that I was to participate in laying some of the first building blocks in the establishment of an important, new university.

And when I told Dr. al-Douri, a few days before I met with him, that I might go abroad on a fellowship, he confirmed to me that he would wait for my return to Baghdad to teach at the College of Arts and Sciences, however long my absence might be.

I was greatly disappointed because the decision of the Council of Higher Education confirmed the fears that I had for several weeks and because it came at a time when my relationship with Lami°a was becoming stronger, and I wanted to marry her without making her lead a wandering, homeless life with me in God's wide world as I looked for a job. But, as it later became clear, my relationship with the woman I loved was the basic motive for making the decision, for it meant that, as soon as my contract ended, I no longer had the right to renew my application to reside in Iraq. A little embarrassed, the dean said, "You and Miss Lami°a, my dear professor, have gone too far in your public appearances together everywhere. I would have wished that you were a little more circumspect."

My answer was simple and reflected the absolute idealism that I could never live without. I said, "I do not do in secret what I am ashamed of in public."

With the wise experience of the administrator who necessarily differentiated between what was practical and what was ideal but impractical in life situations, the dean said, "This is then the result in a society like ours."

After a day or two, I wrote a detailed letter clarifying my position and expressing my deep disappointment with the decision of the Council of Higher Education. I handed it to the dean, and he read it in my presence with clear magnanimity. Then he asked me, "Would you like me to add it to your file?"

I said, "Yes."

And that was the end of the matter.

■ ■ ■

When I told Lami‘a of what had happened, she got angry, but she said that she was not surprised and added, "It is an attempt by certain people to separate us, but it will never succeed." I asked her whether she still wanted to marry me, and she said, "Your question is silly! As if matters like this one could ever shake our determination!"

She told me that the previous night, she contacted her only maternal uncle, Abd al-Hamid Rifat, who was older than her mother. She saw him or his family hardly more than once or twice a year. He had been director general of the Department of the Interior for so many years that nobody could imagine that the state would one day see another director general, on account of his efficiency, his reputation for fairness in a post that had difficult tasks, and his ability—nonetheless—to remain in harmony with every change that occurred in the cabinet. He had chosen a young man as an assistant, in whom he saw signs of ability to follow in his footsteps, namely, Mumtaz al-Umari, cousin of Dr. Isam al-Umari. It seemed that Abd al-Hamid Rifat was about to leave his post, or that he had actually left it by arrangement with the prime minister, to become the legal adviser to the Iraq Petroleum Company, a position that was one of the most important administrative positions in the company and one with close ties to the state because he often would be the one who coordinated the needs of the government and the oil institution.

Lami‘a contacted him by phone and told him about me and who I was. Then she said that we intended to get married shortly and asked him what he thought. Although Abd al-Hamid Rifat was famous for his poise and composure to the extent of being boringly cold, his immediate reply was, "Lami‘a, it is better for you to ask for the moon . . ." And the telephone conversation ended.

I started to describe the situation to her in the darkest colors possible; I said that both of us had little money and that I, as a Palestinian, was being thrown into the cosmic void once more and did not know where I would land . . . As for her, Baghdad was still within her grasp, would she want to risk leaping with me into the unknown?

She said insistently as her deep-black eyes with intensely contrasting whites shone with the flash of her will, "I will stay with you wherever you go. And in the worst of situations, I will consider myself another wandering, homeless Palestinian to be added to the million other such Palestinians."

A few days later, Lami^ca told me that Arshad al-Umari, chairman of the Development Board, said on hearing that my contract was not renewed, "Let him come to me at the board. I think I have an opening that will suit him." And she told me of the appointment he had made to interview me.

At the appointed time, I was surprised to see that man who had been mayor of the capital for many years and played a major role in planning Baghdad, its streets, and its neighborhoods and had created public parks in every part of it—he was originally an architect. He had been a minister more than once and prime minister twice and was now heading the institution considered to be one of the most important in Iraq, for the board would be responsible for spending the greatest part of the rising oil revenues on tens of projects that hundreds of experts were studying and implementing.

I was surprised to see a man of average stature whose age was difficult to determine, and who came to receive me at the door of the building and said humbly, "I am Arshad al-Umari." He led me through the corridors of the building with the determination of a young man in his thirties. He spoke with the fluency and speed of a man who knew exactly where he was going and what he was doing, until we reached his office. It was clear that he was the kind of man who wasted no time with niceties or in trying to impress a visitor that he was one of the most important persons of the state. It seemed that our friend and his son, Dr. Isam al-Umari, had given him as much information as he needed about me, and that Isam, and also his sister Suad, had recommended me to him sufficiently that he offered me a job in a position that required oral and written proficiency in English as well as Arabic.

Then, all of a sudden, he asked, "And what news have you of Lami^ca?"

Before I could answer, he added, "And when will you get married?"

I said, "As soon as our affairs are in order."

He asked, "Are there any difficulties? Any deterrents?"

I said, "Her mother is still hesitant."

He laughed and said, "Umm Amer? A plague on her! Do get married, and I will be the first to bless your wedding. As for Umm Amer, I will persuade her . . . And now, the position and its salary. What was your salary at the College of Arts?"

When I told him, he shook his head and said, "Your income from teaching is higher than the salaries we now offer here. But give me two or three weeks, and good things will come of it."

When I stood up to say goodbye and leave him, he insisted on accompanying me to the door of the building.

(10)

Lami‘a sat on the wide sofa surrounded by many colored cushions. She stretched her legs out comfortably, and Athena brought us coffee, having finally accepted that I had not "smuggled" Lami‘a to my room in order to paint her.

The light of the day was pouring profusely on Lami‘a's face and body from the wide, northern window and playfully shining on her hair and lips, and flashing in her eyes. She was wearing a wine-colored dress, whose neckline revealed her neck and part of her shoulders. I observed the light toying with her dress while she was in that position, and I wished I could paint the scene.

Athena had hardly gone out when she knocked on the door. I quickly went to the door and opened it. As soon as the man she was escorting in saw me, he shouted in an English accent, "Jabra, Jabra!" He shook my hand warmly, adding, "You've not changed a bit!"

I was surprised to see him. I recognized him but for a moment could not remember his name to introduce him to Lami‘a. He said, "Michael Clark . . . Have you forgotten me?"

I then remembered immediately and turned to Lami‘a and said, "Michael Clark . . . Miss Lami‘a al-Askari."

He came closer to the sofa, and she stretched out her graceful hand to him to shake. His face blushed as he said, "Madam, you resemble a legendary queen . . . Semiramis, perhaps?"

"Or the Queen of Sheba," I added. Turning to him, I exclaimed, "Michael Clark in Baghdad! After all these years!"

He said, "I was afraid you've forgotten me . . ."

I said, "How can I forget you in Jerusalem? What year was it? Oh, yes 1945, just before the end of the war. But in those days, I saw you only in your military uniform."

Throughout 1944 and 1945, Jerusalem teemed with British soldiers, a faceless group that was difficult to distinguish one from the other, and one was not concerned to distinguish them. But some high-ranking British officers intentionally wanted to meet as many educated Arabs as possible. My friend Afif Boulus wanted to meet these educated officers too, and he invited some of them to parties at his elegant home in al-Baqa neighborhood, along with a select group of young Arab men and women. He believed at that time that many of those Englishmen would soon have high positions in English political life, and we had to influence them so that they might know that we were a civilized people and rather distinguished, contrary to what the European Jews who often mixed with them suggested. I met Lawrence Durrell at Afif Boulus's home; he had come from Alexandria and was then known only as a poet and had not yet written his *Alexandria Quartet*. I also met Michael Clark, who was then perhaps in his late twenties, while I was twenty-five years of age. He was a quick-witted young man, deeply interested in all he saw and heard and still retained the effects of his years of study at the University of Cambridge in his speech and intonation.

At the time we first met, he had read a poem of mine published in *Forum*, edited by Reggie Smith, the only magazine that appeared in English in Jerusalem. We quickly became friends, especially when I found that he had also gotten acquainted with another friend, Walid al-Khalidi. The three of us met several times, mostly at the home of Walid and his wife, Rasha Salam. Walid, who was in his early twenties, was deeply knowledgeable about English poetry; he was also amazingly fluent in English, although he had not yet gone to study at Oxford.

Michael Clark used to express his amazement whenever he

heard Walid speak with intelligence and vivacity, and he used to look at his handsome face with great admiration and marvel at what he called his "aristocratic" gestures as we spoke about the Palestinian cause, at a time when the Jews had not yet begun their terrorist activities. Michael would say, "Walid is another image of the poet Shelley . . . In fact, he is Shelley himself, don't you think so?" I would agree, and we would talk about the ethereal fire that was always burning in Shelley's eyes and voice, as it was in Walid's eyes and voice at that time.

Michael would say that we were all attracted to wonderful ideals that were the most important basis for the establishment of any young and new state, as the one we dreamed of in Palestine. He would turn to me and say, "And you—you remind me of John the Baptist as he cried in the wilderness to whoever would listen to him . . ." I would laugh and say, "A Brahman friend of mine at Cambridge used to liken me to 'the Light of Asia' at one time, and to the god Vishnu at another . . . and you've not seen anything yet!" Then Rasha would join us with her merry and pleasant comments, followed by Sulafa, Walid's sister, whose complexion was like rose petals, and she would participate in our conversations that soared in limitless space until she would announce that dinner was ready.

And we might visit Walid's father, occupied with his papers in his library, and greet that great man whose graciousness I have never forgotten, from the time I was a student at the Arab College when he was its dean and—at the time—still continued to be: I mean, Ahmad Samih al-Khalidi.

Michael Clark was now here before me in Baghdad! His words sparked with his usual intelligence and exciting comparisons, and he made a point of involving Lamiᶜa in our dialogue, and he called to mind Rasha, Sulafa, and other young women in Jerusalem, whose names had slipped his mind but whose faces he never forgot.

As for me, I did not forget anyone . . . I remembered the Arts Club in Jerusalem, which I headed for some time after we established it in 1944 at the YMCA, and I remembered the tens of lectures and musical recitals that were regular parts of its weekly programs, and the tens of men and women who were an integral part of our cultural life. I remembered Afif Boulus who established the Orpheus Choir, consisting of a large number of young men and women who under his leadership and our club's sponsorship sang choral works and operatic arias that were some of the best in the tradition of classical music. I remembered Salvatore Arnita who participated in our activities with his musical creations and marvelous recitals on the grand organ. I remembered all the people and activities of that exciting and bright period in Jerusalem, before we were unexpectedly invaded by the darknesses of Zionist terror in 1947, which with its malice blew up our vision of all that radiant love.

What I wanted to know now was what had brought Michael Clark to Baghdad and how he had found my apartment. He answered, laughing, "That has a long story. It begins with my release from the army five or six years ago, and then entering a strange world in London, the world of the filmmaking industry."

He had joined a firm known for producing documentary films, which had found that he had a sufficiently broad culture and enthusiasm for the work to encourage it to train him in film production. So he went along with the photographers to the locations and accompanied the sound and montage specialists. He was later trained to write scenarios and discuss them with the person directing the film. Gradually he combined two basic tasks in producing a documentary: first, writing, and then producing what he had written. After the filming was completed and the editing done, he wrote the required narration in the best prose he could command, charging it with poetic power. After the narration was recorded, music that was specially composed for it was added to it.

He thus described for me a cinematic procedure that I knew nothing about. I did not know that I would be lured into it so strongly two or three years later that I would remain occupied with it for many years afterwards as another means of expression, besides writing and painting, and sometimes no less exciting to my imagination and pleasure.

The new oil agreement had brought Michael Clark to

Baghdad. The Iraq Petroleum Company had laid a huge pipeline from Kirkuk in Iraq to the Syrian port of Banyas on the Mediterranean Sea. This raised the rate of oil production phenomenally and, as a consequence, it raised the amount of Iraq's oil revenue, based on the recently agreed up one-half share, whereas the country's share earlier had been only four gold shillings for every ton of oil extracted.

I did not know what Michael Clark intended by giving me all this information, which was not exactly of direct interest to me. Then he suddenly said, "I have produced a documentary film on the construction of this pipeline. It took me many months to make, here and in Syria as well as in London. I have written narration for it—in English, of course."

I said, "Congratulations. But why has all this brought you to me here today?"

He said, "The important thing about my film is that the narration on it should be in Arabic, and not in English. So I asked Frank Stokes—you know him, no doubt?"

I was not sure at first; then I remembered meeting him more than once in our musical evenings at the College of Arts. My friend continued, "I asked him where I could find a good writer here, with a modern outlook, etc. . . . and he immediately replied, 'I know a professor at the College of Arts named So-and-So.' I was thunderstruck. You were here in Baghdad, while I have been here all these months and had no idea ? We immediately began making inquiries and someone told me you are well known at the Sindbad Hotel. A waiter from the Sindbad Hotel led me right to the door of your apartment, as you can see."

The result was that we agreed that I would translate the narration into Arabic. We then made sure that my Arabic text was suitable, so I read what I had written as the film was shown without sound. The important thing about the project was how enjoyable our meetings were; sometimes Lami^ca was with us, and Michael spoke about the latest trends in poetry and fiction in England. During all this, I met Frank Stokes more than once and found in him an enjoyable blend of seriousness and sharp humor. Meanwhile, the hot Iraqi summer was lazily advancing in its own

way as I waited for a letter from John Marshall that would determine whether or not I would travel to the United States.

■　■　■

We spent most evenings in groups, either in the garden of
Qahtan Awni's home or Husayn Haddawi's. Each of the two
friends had his own group, but Lamiᶜa and I were common to
both. Then there were the long-lasting evenings in the open cafés
on the banks of the Tigris on Abou Nuwas Street. We often organized the preparation of fish grilled on wooden stakes *(mazqouf)*
on one of the river's "islands," sand bars that appeared when the
water receded in the summer and could be reached by boat,
where many people spent the hot evenings eating and drinking.
People appeared to be unable to live without those small islands
created by nature in the right season. Many people who had the
financial means erected shacks *(jaradigh,* singular *jurdagh)* on
them. Usually put up on the Karkh side of the Tigris bank, they
were light open shacks similar to primitive huts, but they were
sufficient for the needs of long evening parties.

One day Amer came to Baghdad on a short vacation from
his work in the Zammar subdistrict in northern Iraq and invited
me to lunch at home. Before we entered the dining room and
as Lamiᶜa and her mother and Umm Shakir were busy preparing the table, I said to Amer, "You have been away from us for a
long time. It seems that you prefer your northern region to
Baghdad because of its cool weather these days . . . Amer, you
may not know that I consider Lamiᶜa the most wonderful young
woman in my life."

He said, laughing, "By God, I too consider my sister the most
wonderful young woman I have known in my life."

I said, "That is why and in confirmation of your words and
mine, I am honored and happy to ask for her hand."

I kept silent, waiting for his response, while he continued
to look at me without saying anything. Then he got up, held my
head between his hands, and kissed me on the forehead, saying,
"With my blessings."

Lamiᶜa did not know what happened until we finished eating

lunch and each of us wanted to go and have a nap. Lami^ca walked with me to the outside door to say goodbye. I said to her, "Congratulations! You are now my fiancée, formally." And I told her what had happened.

Surprised, she erupted, pulled me by the hand back inside. She called Amer and asked, "Why didn't you tell me, you traitor!" He held her head between his hands as he had held mine and kissed her forehead saying, "Congratulations, my dear."

On her part, she broke into tears and called her mother, "Mama! The engagement has happened!"

A few days later, John Marshall's letter finally arrived, conveying to me all the necessary details about my acceptance at Harvard, my journey by sea to New York and hence by train to Boston. All I had to do was to go to the Thomas Cook Travel Agency, to the very same Mr. Samuel, my good-hearted neighbor who had arranged my trip to Paris a year earlier.

The ship that was to carry me from Beirut across the Mediterranean then the Atlantic Ocean was called *Muhammad Ali al-Kabir* of the Khedival Lines. A deluxe cabin was reserved for me. But how could I now add to the reservation the lady who would become my wife in a few days? The fare would be doubled, and that was not within our financial means. Besides, the deluxe cabins were few and had been all reserved.

At this juncture, Mr. Samuel saved us with his experience. "Why should you bear the double expense when I can reserve a third-class cabin for Mrs. Lami^ca at the cheapest fare, only ninety dinars? All you have to do when you board the ship is to go directly to the deluxe cabin already reserved for you. It has its own bathroom and complete privacy. You can both stay in it . . . I'll take care of that, Professor."

Two or three days later, I took Husayn Haddawi to Mr. Samuel so that he might make reservations on the same ship for himself, his wife, and his daughter Maryam. We later learned that meals were the same for all classes in one large dining hall on board, and thus we could stay in continual touch with one another throughout the long three-week journey.

At that time, the Revolution of July 2 3 took place in Egypt, and it occupied us all as well as the whole world. It surprised us and made us rejoice, for it took place without the shedding of a single drop of blood. But I was afraid that our reservation on board the *Muhammad Ali al-Kabir* might be affected. So I hurried to Mr. Samuel to inquire about the matter, but he reassured me that everything was fine and that the Khedival Lines were international and not easily affected by local events. He also said that we would find that the captain of the ship and his crew were all Greek anyway and that seafaring was their profession and they were all well-trained and well-mannered.

(11)

When I decided that the ninth of August would be the day of our wedding (I was born in August, and it has always been a month of blessings for me), I felt a great internal peace reign within me after several months of painful, emotional struggle.

The sweltering heat was scorching Baghdad's buildings and melting the asphalt of its streets. We went to a jeweler near the Mackenzie Bookstore on a little street branching off of al-Rashid Street. We ordered two wedding rings and asked the jeweler to engrave the date 9-8-1952 on the inside of each. We then walked to the Swiss Café to have coffee. I felt so buoyant in my movement and in my soul that I felt I could fly if I wanted. Lamiᶜa appeared to me like a Babylonian goddess who could lead me to the depths of the underworld, as Astarte did, in order to bring out Tammuz with us as we ascended, and we would be stronger and more eager to proceed to wider horizons, where I could in turn lead her to where God had created paradises and welcomed whomever He wanted, among those He loved and who loved Him.

I noticed that Lamiᶜa, like me and my mother, did not wear gold jewelry such as bracelets, necklaces, and other embellishments, for she always insisted on remaining without such adornments. The exception was that she wore earrings but avoided those made of gold. She told me that her family had inherited a lot of jewelry, some from her uncle Bakr Sidqi. Her mother gave her that jewelry when she was a student at Teachers' College. Instead of wearing it, Lami‘a sold it one piece at a time and bought chocolate bars and kilograms of nuts with the money, and thus she dissipated all her gold inheritance. She would not allow me to buy her any gold jewelry, not even a single symbolic piece, other than the wedding ring.

As we were at the café talking about her aversion to gold, I said that I preferred silver because of its whiteness and purity; then I added, jokingly, "But unfortunately, I was not born with a silver spoon in my mouth!"

She laughed and said, looking intently into my eyes, "But you were born with something more precious and rare in your mouth . . . You were born with a silver tongue in your mouth."

"How sweet your bias in favor of me is!" I said. I then remembered the deprivation that I had experienced in my childhood and that, unconsciously at the time, I had not allowed to affect my attitude to life. I mentioned to Lami‘a that, after my return from Cambridge, my mother always gave me a special knife and fork when she set the table. At first I did not notice that they were different from the cutlery used by the other family members. My knife and fork, I later realized, were of silver! When I asked my mother about that, she said, "Don't you know, then? . . ." And she told me that, during the time I spent studying abroad, the family had gone through difficult and lean years but that she managed to save enough money to buy a silver knife and fork for my use when I returned. That was her gift to me, she explained . . . and she continued to insist in the following years that no one should use them but me. Whenever I returned home from Baghdad, my mother brought them out and polished them until they shone and put them on the table for me to use at mealtime . . . What love could ever be sweeter and more tender than that?

After coffee, Lami‘a and I left the Swiss Café and went out into Baghdad's glare. We strolled along the colonnaded sidewalk of al-Rashid Street and saw a man with a pushcart selling yellow-green apples. We bought a bagful from him then rode the first two-horse carriage that came our way. I said to the coachman, "Keep going on your way!" Lami‘a put the bag of apples in her lap, and with the rhythmic sound of the horses' hoofs striking the road, we gradually ate the apples, whose Baghdadi acidity I loved.

Suddenly Lami^ca laughed and said, "With only one apple, Eve expelled Adam from Paradise. Here I am offering you twenty apples! Woe be to you from me!"

I said, "Eve did indeed cause Adam to be expelled from Paradise with one big apple, but with twenty little ones you are returning him to Paradise anew! And what a return!"

We did not know whether the coachman listened to what we were saying, but we were not concerned with whether he was or not. He went on smoking freely, and we continued to talk freely too, and the two horses trotted lazily in the damn heat to wherever they were going until, an hour later, we found that we had reached the outskirts of New Baghdad. At that point, I said to the coachman, "Now take us back to al-Rashid Street, God bless you!"

Who in the world would go out in the noon heat of blazing August to have a ride on the streets of Baghdad and flirt? Who, except the two of us? What did we say and what did we keep unsaid for coming days?

I usually told Lami^ca many jokes, mostly in English and of the sort that only English people might appreciate, for they consider one's sense of humor as important in life as the sun and the air. However, on that day I told her that after marriage I would ration the store of jokes I still had and that I would tell her only two jokes per day. Would she accept? She accepted, reluctantly! The ability to tell a story or relate something well, whatever it might be, was one of my qualities that attracted her. One day she said to me, "Do you know something? I have now discovered a secret that I must reveal to you. What attracted me to you was not only your learning, your art, your literature, your vivacity—all of which are fine and dandy—but rather your skill in relating things, a story, an event, a joke, whether in Arabic or in English . . . You make everything you say important and exciting, whether it is small or great, real or fabricated . . . You make all life seem important and exciting: what a wonderful illusionist I have married!"

■   ■   ■

161

At nine o'clock in the morning of the ninth day of August, I was looking out of my wide northern window to the street, waiting for Hilmi who had promised to come in his little, red convertible. I remembered how many important stages of my life this wonderful friend had shared with me since the time we were students together at the Arab College, followed in the fall of 1939 by our sea journey to England during part of which we faced the dangers of the Atlantic Ocean when it was mercilessly stormy for many days in the Bay of Biscay . . . Memories were numerous: from Jerusalem to England, and back again to Jerusalem, then to Baghdad where we both taught at its colleges. Then there was that beautiful experience that lasted for more than a year in the company of male and female friends, at the center of whom were Lami^{c}a for me and for him wonderful Evelyn, Lami^{c}a's friend who was professor of psychology at Queen Aliya College and daughter of one of the most famous medical specialists in Baghdad. All indications pointed to the fact that, like us, Hilmi and Evelyn would soon get married despite certain difficulties. Yet, with all his obvious genius in mathematics and physics, Hilmi's contract had not been renewed, and he was obliged to look for another job in Iraq, where he had settled with his father's family in the autumn of 1948.

I noticed Hilmi's car and saw him park it. He raised his head and looked at my window. I opened it, waved to him, and closed it. Then I hurried downstairs as his engine was still roaring. I sat next to him and we drove on al-Rashid Street to Husayn Haddawi's home near the Iron Bridge.

Husayn and his wife Krista insisted that we should get out and have a cup of coffee at their home before going to Lami^{c}a's. Krista said to me in English, "You must be very excited. Did you imagine, four years ago, when you came to Baghdad as a stranger whom no one knew, that you would one day marry one of the most beautiful young women of the city?"

Half an hour later, I sat next to Hilmi in his car, and Husayn sat behind us in the narrow rumble seat. We drove to Lami^{c}a's home on Taha Street as the day was becoming hotter and hotter. The convertible did not protect us from the stinging rays of the sun, although the breeze that blew on us as we drove comforted us a little. Minutes later, Lami‘a and her mother welcomed us, and we all sat in the drawing room with its large green armchairs, and Umm Shakir brought us tea in little glasses.

When we finally stood up to leave, I saw Lami‘a go to her mother and embrace her, saying, "Mama, bless my marriage now. I will not move on until you give me your blessing."

Her mother kissed her warmly and said, "May it be blessed. Congratulations, my sweetheart. I was always afraid that this friend of yours would take from me the only creature for whom I lived and for whom I would die. And he has now done it!" She then approached me, and I kissed her cheeks as she said to me, "Congratulations and may you both have all the best, God willing."

We went back to the red car. Husayn and I crowded together in the rumble seat and Lami‘a sat next to Hilmi who, taking his curved pipe out of his mouth for a moment and blowing a cloud of smoke from it, shouted, "Let's go." And we drove to the Sunni court on River Street.

I had witnessed many marriages and weddings before, and since that day, I have witnessed dozens of others that filled the world with music and song, and engagement, dowry, and wedding parties as well, including the parties that years later my wife and I gave our two sons, Sadeer and Yasser, in accordance with their wishes, in fulfillment of the desires of their brides and their families and in agreement with social conventions. We enjoyed those parties very much, but our own marriage differed from all these. Ours was a marriage of a man and a woman who had chosen each other to the exclusion of everyone else and who had not sought the permission or actual help of anyone else—other than the blessings of a number of loving people and friends. We made a point of ignoring certain people who, we were aware, had openly or secretly expressed their disapproval of our marriage. I had never known a marriage like ours, for it was realized by our own will and not by the will of any other human being. When we entered the old building that the court was in, I felt how fair and how humane this law *(sharia)* was; for a man and a woman to marry only required that each of them should accept the other and that two witnesses be present to testify to that.

We were wearing the most simple clothes: Lami°a wore a white blouse with short sleeves and a wide neckline, a gray skirt, and low-heeled shoes (she always preferred not to wear high heels except when necessary at evening parties); and I wore a white shirt with an open collar, and trousers that were gray too. At any rate, does the August heat in Baghdad allow other than that or more than it?

As soon as judge Abd al-Hamid al-Atrushi saw me, he welcomed me for I had become Muslim at his hands a few days earlier, and he had not forgotten me. After being introduced to Lami°a and the two witnesses and after reading the forms which we had filled out, he noticed the amount of the bride's dowry mentioned in the marriage certificate he was to sign. He raised his head and asked, "Lami°a Barqi Shawqi al-Askari: do you know that your immediate dowry is one dinar and that your delayed dowry is two dinars?"

She answered, "Yes, your honor."

He asked, "And are you satisfied with this dowry?"

She said, "Yes, I'm satisfied."

He asked, "And have you received the one dinar as an immediate dowry?"

She said, "Yes."

While smiling, he looked from her to me, then from one witness to the other. Then he said, "I testify by God that this marriage is not motivated by money."

He quickly concluded what he had to do; the two witnesses signed the document, and I received it. The judge congratulated us and bade us farewell with marked cheerfulness, for he had seen that morning what he did not see every day: a marriage of two lovers.

We crowded in the little car again. Hilmi and Husayn insisted that the newly married couple should sit together in the rumble seat behind them. We both wore our wedding rings, and I said, "Now, to the Sindbad Hotel for lunch."

When the two waiters, Hanna and Ilyas, in the hotel's dining room learned that we had just gotten married, they provided us with the most delicious food they had, including grilled pheasant with which they usually spoiled their favored customers. We each ordered a double glass of Rémy Martin cognac, which was my favorite drink and Hilmi's. When we drank a toast to our marriage, Lami‘a tasted cognac for the first—and last—time in her life; she took a very little sip then pushed the glass away from her. As for us men, we drank it along with other drinks we later ordered. After lunch, we headed for a lounge where a so-called air conditioner was trying hard to cool the place but succeeded only in increasing the humidity of the air as we sweated profusely. There was nobody in the lounge but us, for everyone was having a midday nap, whereas we alone constantly talked and laughed. Then they brought us tea and, at that moment, it seemed to us that it tasted as delicious as the Rémy Martin.

■　■　■

A day or two later, my faithful female student who had graduated with distinction in English literature was able to get in touch with me to thank me for responding to her desire that I return her letters. (I wonder, what does a woman do with letters that she wrote day after day with her heart's blood when they are suddenly returned to her in one bundle?) She congratulated me on my marriage and sent me an expensive gift: a gold cigarette box with a map of Iraq engraved inside. I don't usually carry a box of this sort, especially if it is made of gold, and I smoke only a few cigarettes per day because I constantly smoke a pipe. However, I was greatly moved, and I appreciated that beautiful gift from her. I wondered: Should I mention it to Lami‘a? I decided not to, and kept the cigarette box among my many belongings. The strange thing was that it disappeared. I never knew how and when it disappeared, and whether Lami‘a had a role in its disappearance but did not tell me. Naturally I did not mention its disappearance to anyone.

■　■　■

After our memorable day, we had nothing to do but prepare ourselves for the journey to the United States. Our ship was to leave Beirut early in September. I had first to go to Bethlehem to see my mother and my two brothers, Yousuf and Murad. One of the last things I did in Baghdad was to make sure that my brother Isa had rented a new residence at al-Nasr Square, to which he would move my library and my paintings soon after my departure.

One afternoon, Lami‘a and I went up to the top floor of Orozdy Bak on al-Rashid Street so that I might buy her a dress. We chose an azure-blue dress, and when she tried it on and came out from behind the curtain of the fitting room, we both went crazy about it. Lami‘a's dark Baghdad complexion used to be transformed into an amazing brilliance with certain colors she wore. Turquoise, light blue, and pink were some of the colors that ignited that magic charm of hers, which emphasized the gleam of her eyes and the gracefulness of her body and its plump curves. Lami‘a considered that dress to be my gift to her on the occasion of our wedding, and she refused that I buy her anything else (until the ship carried us a few days later to a number of Italian ports, where the lure of buying was more enticing and her response to it was stronger).

My plan was that she should precede me by going to Beirut a day or two before I did and stay at the home of Aliya al-Umari's brother, Nathir al-Umari and his wife Mayy. In those days, Nathir was first or second secretary at the Iraqi embassy there. Then I would come by airplane from Jerusalem after spending about ten days with my family in Bethlehem.

In those exciting hours in Baghdad, we did not forget that Lami‘a had to be released from her position by making an arrangement with her college and the Ministry of Education. She made efforts to that effect and met with the minister and informed him of her marriage to me. She requested his approval for what is administratively called "a leave without pay" in order to accompany me during my studies in the United States. The minister surprised her by giving his unhesitating approval for her to be absent for one year, and he would continue her salary until he could consider the matter later.

In Bethlehem I spent enjoyable days with my mother and with Yousuf and Murad, and their families. Many friends and acquaintances came to visit us, but I did not tell my relatives about my marriage in order to avoid any possibility for needless conflict. I went out for long walks to Duhaysha, al-Khadir, and Solomon's Pools with my brothers and with several of my old friends; we also visited the old city of Jerusalem and its eastern suburbs as I usually did when I returned from Baghdad to Bethlehem after a long absence.

On the afternoon before the day of my departure, I was going up the stairs in the municipal market when a woman coming down the stairs met me and greeted me warmly. She was one of my mother's longtime friends and was one of our neighbors at Jawrat al-Nisnas in Jerusalem. Her name was Warda and she surprised me by saying, "I heard that you got married."

"And who told you that?" I asked evasively and in astonishment.

She said, "I heard that you have married the daughter of a pasha in Baghdad. Do you remember what I told you when I read your coffee cup three or four years ago, during one of your visits from Baghdad?"

Warda was known for her skill in "reading" coffee cups and spared no opportunity to demonstrate this skill. When I showed no sign of remembering what she had told me when she read my coffee cup three or four years earlier, she volunteered the details. I was amazed that, having read hundreds of other people's coffee cups since that day, she still remembered what she had seen in my cup.

"Have you forgotten?" she began. "Well let me remind you. We were at Khamis's home, with such and such persons. We drank coffee and you said to me, 'Aunt Warda, please read my cup . . .' My goodness! What a wonderful cup it was that I saw in my hands. Do you remember? I saw a pile of chairs, one chair on top of another and yet another and another. On the very top of these chairs, on the tip-top, there was a big chair on which you, my darling, were sitting. What? Have you forgotten? By God, I haven't. I told your mother at the time, I said to her, 'Your son is going to reach a high place, a very very high place . . . '"

167

I remembered then that she had read my cup, but her excessive enthusiasm made me laugh; for I have never thought of sitting on any of the chairs that interested my aunt Warda. When I told her that I remembered, she said, "Yesterday, when they told me that you married a daughter of a pasha, I said to them, 'By God, I was the one who told him so, years ago' . . . Yet, my darling, what is to come is still much greater . . . Tomorrow I'll visit your mother in the afternoon and we'll drink coffee at your home, and you'll see . . . At any rate, go in peace now and give my greetings to your mother."

She continued her way down the stairs, and I thanked God that when she would come on the next day, I would be in the air on an airplane going to Beirut.

■ ■ ■

The airplane landed at the Beirut airport. I had sent a telegram to Nathir al-Umari in which I told him about the date and time of my arrival. My heart throbbed violently as I wanted the passport and customs procedures to end quickly, and I looked in the distance toward the long concourse leading to the exit. In spite of the bad lighting and the fall of night outside, I noticed a graceful figure standing in the middle of the lobby among many people hurrying in and out. I immediately knew that it was Lamiᶜa. She was wearing a white outfit that I had not seen her wear before, and it shone brightly and lit all the hall. I saw no one else but her. I ran toward her as the porter ran behind me with his cart carrying my bags. I took her in my arms like a madman . . . then she said, "Here is the driver, waiting for us. Emile?"

Emile came forward and shook hands with me; then he led us to the car. The car was of course Nathir's, and Emile was his chauffeur. He put my luggage in the car's trunk and tipped the porter himself. He then drove us through the streets of the city, which was one of three or four cities that I loved and will continue to love as long as I live.

After the cool weather of the hills of Jerusalem and Bethlehem, Beirut in the summer was not only hot but also very humid. In Baghdad, before midnight, a cool desert breeze blows; but in Beirut, the hot humidity of the sea does not diminish, even as night advances.

Nathir and Mayy gave us their apartment, which opened on the sea and was close to the Rawsheh (Rocher). They rented a house in Souq al-Gharb on Mount Lebanon for the rest of the summer. But after the chauffeur said goodbye to us, Lamiᶜa and I found that the air in the apartment was unbearably muggy, even after we had opened all the windows. (In those days, air conditioning was not yet prevalent.) We remained awake until morning —although the heat was only a secondary reason for our lack of sleep, given our love and the fact that that was the first whole night we had spent together.

No sooner had the first rays of the sun begun to shine on the waves than we finished with our breakfast and morning coffee. We closed the windows, left the apartment with our luggage and locked the door. A taxi immediately approached, and carried our luggage and us up to Aley on the mountain and hence to Souq al-Gharb, where the driver brought us to the address that Lamiᶜa had given him for Nathir and Mayy's house.

And what a beautiful couple I saw there!

If love sometimes occurs at first sight, certain friendships are like love and are born at first sight too. The intimate relationship that immediately arose between me and these two persons was just like that. No doubt, the words that each of us had earlier heard spoken about the other had had their effect, although the expectations raised by what one hears about others may at times end in bitter disappointment.

Nathir was my age or perhaps older by one or two years despite the early gray that was making inroads in his hair. Like me, he had studied in England during the war and returned to Iraq with great difficulty, exactly at the same time that I returned to Jerusalem with similar difficulty.

Mayy was his cousin, and I found out that she was several years younger than he was—she was also younger than Lamiᶜa. With her rosy complexion, thick blond hair, and large blue eyes, no one would ever have believed that she was an Iraqi from Mosul. It was not difficult for me to realize that this rare pearl was one day the focus of rivalry between her male cousins until Nathir won her when she was sixteen years old, a short while after his return from study abroad; and for years, Lamiᶜa had been the center of their interest.

At that time I understood the secret of the great attraction between Lamiᶜa and the members of this distinguished family: it was their vivacity, coupled with their immense intellectual openness and generosity of spirit and added to that was the fact that some individuals among them were endowed with an unusual quality that placed them together in a special category of people. By their clear intelligence, their lively intellect, their varied education, their eloquence and their inner pride, they formed a cohesive group regardless of whether there existed a blood relationship or not. That may have been the reason that I was attracted to them and they to me, although I was not aware of it at the time. This attraction made me feel—or it was they who inspired me to feel—that deep inside we all belonged together and that we did not need to speak about it.

I soon discovered that Nathir's hobby was painting, especially in water colors which he used with skilful transparency. Years later in the middle 1960s, when he had become Iraqi ambassador in Beirut, it was fitting that, upon my insistence, he exhibited his paintings at Gallery One that was run by my dear friend, poet Yousuf al-Khal. His paintings, which portrayed the Lebanese landscape that we all loved, received an acclaim that only professional artists receive.

We spent the morning with Nathir and Mayy and had lunch with them, and questions and answers about our private life and public matters continued. The tender and cool air of Souq al-Gharb reminded me of the air of the hills of Jerusalem and Bethlehem that are exactly the same height as those of Souq al-Gharb.

After four o'clock in the afternoon, Nathir took us in his car to the Grand Kamel Hotel, which was the most modern and the biggest hotel in town; it overlooked the slopes of the mountain descending gradually toward Beirut and the sea; and beyond Beirut, the sea shone with its foggy blue and stretched toward the distant horizon in the west.

We liked the hotel and wanted to reserve a room in it for Lami^{c}a and me, but it was full. The hotel owners suggested that we stay at the hotel next door, the Sursuq Hotel, which also had the view from the hilltop but was an older hotel. So after having tea in the parlor of the Kamel Hotel, we went to the Sursuq Hotel where we were lucky to get a good room and decided to remain in it until the time we would board the ship, three or four days later. It must be said that, in later years until 1974, few were the summers that we did not spend wholly or mostly in the Kamel Hotel at Souq al-Gharb, and it was as though we were members of the family in our relations with its good-hearted owners. However, we stopped going to Lebanon after the tragic civil war which started there in the spring of 1975, exactly as we had earlier stopped going to Bethlehem and Jerusalem in June of 1967, when Israel occupied all of Palestine. This was a painful deprivation to us and to millions of Arabs, and it reminds us at every moment of the tragedies that have continued to pursue this Arab nation like some crazy fate.

But between the summers of 1952 and 1974, we had more than two decades full of lively experiences in Lebanon with its mountain and shores. Lami^{c}a and I came to know many exciting people there and various kinds of friendship and love as well as intellectual and creative activity that gave our life—my life in particular—some of its most beautiful experiences and some of its most enjoyable inspiration. Had it not been for Beirut, even in the terrible years that followed, our life would have been poorer and would have lost much of its sweetness and ecstasy.

In the forenoon of the following day, Imad al-Umari, Isam's younger brother and Nathir's cousin, surprised us by driving from Damascus to congratulate us. He said that he had to go back that night because he could not obtain a leave from his job for more than twenty-four hours and that was why he could not bring along his wife, Salma, with him—they were newly married. Imad radiated so much merriment, laughter, and geniality, he could have been Lami^{c}a's brother. He continued to be a dear brother to both of us for many years, some of which was not without sorrow and pain. We invited him with his Syrian wife to visit us at Harvard as soon as we were settled there. (He and Salma accepted our invitation in the following summer and came to Harvard and stayed in our little apartment; we all slept on blankets spread on the floor and were as happy as though we slept on beds made of ostrich feathers!)

In the morning of the third day, we left the Sursuq Hotel and went to the Thomas Cook Travel Agency in Beirut to make sure of the departure time of the *Muhammad Ali al-Kabir*. We dropped by the post office, and I sent a telegram to John Marshall in New York informing him that I had gotten married a few days earlier and that my wife was accompanying me on the journey and would live with me at Harvard, and I told him that we would arrive in New York on such and such a day.

We then returned to Martyrs' Square, which in those days was perhaps the most marvelous square in any city in the world with its people, movement, noise, and color. We went to the al-Buhsali's pastry shop to buy two large boxes of baklava, ballouriyya, and burma. Without discussion, we believed in the verse composed more than twenty years earlier by another lover of al-Buhsali's pastries, the Prince of Poets, Ahmad Shawqi, a verse which the owner of the shop had printed in beautiful calligraphy on the blue paper with which the boxes were wrapped. The verse says:

> Talk of the sweetness of two things:
> The beloved's mouth and al-Buhsali's pastry.

Some pieces of this baklava and ballouriyya would help in persuading the Greek sailor in charge of the deluxe cabin reserved for me on board the *Muhammad Ali al-Kabir* to move me from my single room to a double room, worthy of two lovers spending their honeymoon on the waves of the Mediterranean Sea and the Atlantic Ocean, who it was clear to all possessed nothing of the world's chattel but themselves and their love—and some of al-Buhsali's pastries.

(12)

That was my fifth journey by sea and the most enjoyable and eventful of them all. My first had taken place exactly thirteen years earlier, in 1939, when I went to England by way of Port Said in the company of Hilmi Samara and Hamid Attari. That was the first time I had left my country, and the Second World War had just begun. Behind me, I had left people whom I loved and who loved me, as I embarked on an adventure to unknown regions where I began discovering my relationship with the wider world through books, art, and love, hoping I would discover unknown regions within myself. Every leg of the journey, every port we visited, every wave that toyed with us before hurling us away with the violence of a volcano, aroused in me an innate yearning that would later lead me to enter the tumult of humanity and nature, of reason and feeling, of knowledge and emotion, all of which would continue to lead me forward through the following years.

My second journey took place four years afterward, when I was twenty-three and had finished my studies at Cambridge and departed from the port of Liverpool as German bombs were falling. By what scheme and what folly had I decided to undertake the odyssey of returning to my country! Having been among the first five in the examinations of the tripos in English literature among a large number of British students, the director of education in Palestine suggested to William Thatcher, the dean of my college, that I should continue my studies for three more years and obtain a doctorate. I refused and insisted on returning to Jerusalem because "I wanted to write" as I said to the dean with the special affection that had grown between him and me. He always said to me as he observed my capricious study habits and other whims throughout the previous three years, "I want you to work like a doltish English horse and not like a fiery Arabian steed." I told him that the demon of writing had possessed me, and I wanted to spend all my hours with him: "I cannot spend three more years studying some writer. I want to devote myself wholly to write about what I myself feel and think." The dean did not know the extent of my eagerness to see my family nor my deep sense that I would die at the age of twenty-six and that I had to hurry up to realize in words the poems, the visions, and the follies that seethed in my heart. Neither did the dean know what a beautiful woman I would leave behind me as I embarked on an adventure toward unknown regions that mercilessly called out to me as I crossed the ocean again toward my dream.

The journey on the Atlantic Ocean lasted thirty days, during which we saw nothing but water and sky. We were in a flotilla of ships of which my ship was the smallest, yet it was their leader. That was its maiden voyage, and it had thirteen passengers on board, a fact that made us consider the captain's cat the fourteenth out of fear of the ill-omened number 13. We were right to be afraid, for the depths of the ocean were plied by German submarines well known in that year, 1943, for having destroyed many British ships. We were attacked at least two or three times, and the warships protecting the flotilla shot depth charges into the ocean. We would rise to the top of the mountainous waves then descend into the valleys between. I saw the waves sometimes rise like giants of legend, roaring and angrily tossing the ship with each surge; and I also saw them calm and peacefully sleeping, murmuring as they stretched endlessly, smooth as a desert of oil, on which shone phosphorescent stars in the moonlight, and it was as though we were sailing on a vast lake . . . I saw the ocean with its incredible, dreamy beauty and I saw it with its hateful, fierce rancor. This reminded me of much English poetry inspired by the seas—especially Coleridge's "The Rime of the Ancient Mariner." I too wrote poems while on the ocean as we descended from the northern hemisphere toward the equator and anchored on the African coast at Lagos in Nigeria.

My third journey by sea took place eight years later, the previous summer, when I went to Paris by way of Marseilles, having gone there from Beirut and Baghdad. That was really a pleasure cruise, but it was the time when, with Lamiᶜa waiting for me in Baghdad, I examined my emotions for her through the summer months. Or was it that she was examining both her emotions and mine?

My later return by sea from Marseilles to Beirut was my fourth journey. The strange thing about it is that, radiant as my memories of the Mediterranean and its ports were in the previous journey, the return journey on the same sea did not leave any real memories—except the bright day I spent on Aphrodite's island, Cyprus; the reason is that it was a fast journey this time, and I wanted nothing but to arrive in Baghdad to see Lami ͨa.

And here I was now on my fifth journey by sea, and my wife was finally with me and nothing else in life concerned me. By sailing along the coasts, by visiting the Greek, Italian, and French ports and finally the port of Gibraltar on our way, and just before going west across the Atlantic Ocean to the port of New York, I felt that our lives, Lami ͨa's and mine, were now beginning anew, very much as my own life had when sailing on this same sea on my way to England for university studies. This then was the beginning of a second stage, for which the first stage with all its experiences, pleasures, and pains was but preparation. This was a second birth, and other wonderful experiences, pleasures, and pains would be realized in it. It is as though our first life existed only to make the second very much richer.

The Italian cities that I had seen on my previous journeys appeared now more beautiful and significant. Centuries of modern history appeared to us to be radiant with what we knew about art and what we had read in English literature. We landed, and sometimes lingered, in Palermo, Naples, Sorento, the Isle of Capri, Genoa, Livorno, and Pisa. My old infatuation with the poet Shelley returned to me in Livorno, and I imagined him sailing far into the sea on his boat *Ariel,* full of ebullient emotions and explosive visions, to drown during a violent summer squall when he was only thirty years of age, a little younger than I; the waves carried him back to the shore, where his friend Byron supervised the burning of his body, fueling the blaze by pouring wine on the fire, glass after glass, then finding that Shelley's heart resisted the fire, which was unable to consume it! How beautiful that shore was, and how large the squares of the city were, and how tender its air was wherever we walked or sat down, remembering those events!

From Livorno we went to Pisa to see its striped marble church and leaning tower. We ascended the hundreds of steps to the top of the tower, where the bells were crowded. We wished we could go from there to Venice, but our ship was scheduled to leave from Livorno that night. Yet the mere mention of Venice aroused in Lami'a the remembrance of the Bridge of Sighs in it.

Suddenly she asked me, "But do you know where the House of Sighs is?"

I laughed and said, "Certainly it is not in Venice."

"Of course not," she said, "it is in Baghdad, on al-Rashid Street, and you don't know . . . It is the house that you lived in."

"I don't understand," I said.

"Whenever I passed with my friends by the house, on the top floor of which was your apartment, I used to look up to your window and sigh! Aliya noticed that more than once, and she called it 'The House of Sighs' . . . And so, every time we passed by it, we used to stop for a couple of moments and sigh together . . ."

I shouted, "My God! You've loved me all this time, and I did not know!"

And I gave her a long kiss on her cheek for everyone to see.

■ ■ ■

When we anchored in New York, we were received by an employee of the Rockefeller Foundation, who carried a large bouquet of white roses that he gave to Lami'a. He congratulated us on our marriage and gave me a letter from John Marshall welcoming both of us and giving us the address of one of Harvard University's institutions, where we should go upon our arrival in Cambridge and stay until we found an apartment to live in permanently. With the help of the Rockefeller employee, our luggage was collected. He had reserved seats for us on the train going to Boston that afternoon. He gave us detailed information on things we needed, provided us with addresses and necessary telephone numbers and did not leave us until he saw the train move northwards with us on it.

When we left the train in Boston and were leaving the railway station with a cart behind us with our luggage being pushed by a porter, I noticed that there was a man near us. He was about fifty years old, and his face and smart clothes gave the impression that he was a wealthy and respected man. Next to him was an ostentatiously and luxuriously dressed lady and surrounding them as they left the train were porters carrying their baggage.

As Lami‘a and I walked together, the man came close to her while his wife was on his other side. I was astonished by his familiarity as he began to talk to Lami‘a. I did not hear what he first said, but then I saw him take her arm and say to her, "Don't be afraid, my sweetheart. All arrangements have been made . . . and the car is waiting for us there . . ."

I had no other choice but to snatch Lami‘a's arm and take her away from him, saying to her in English, "Don't listen to him! He's a madman." Lami‘a did not understand what was happening.

The lady turned to me angrily and said, "Sir, the man you called a madman happens to be my husband."

I furiously retorted, "Madam, if the man is your husband, why don't you take him away from my wife?"

The man said nothing but he smiled and gently waved his hand to Lami‘a as his wife dragged him by the arm, saying, "Look where you're walking, for Christ's sake!" And they went away to their car.

Lami‘a and I burst out laughing as she said, "We've hardly stepped on American soil . . ."

We settled in Cambridge, Massachusetts, in a house at 60 Ellery Street owned by a used-furniture merchant named Henry Fournier, whose hobby was playing the violin with two or three musicians in his apartment on the top floor of the house. He was a man past fifty, rather a bohemian, whose wife had abandoned him. He did not interfere with the affairs of those who lived in his apartments, which he furnished from his shop full of all kinds of used chairs, beds, and mirrors. As long as we did not complain of his playing the violin and cello with his friends in his nest on the top floor, he did not object to any sound or noise from our apartments, whether it was music, a heated argument, or a scream in a quarrel.

The apartment next to us would be occupied, through our mediation, by Dr. Sami al-Shaykh Qasim and his wife Mayy Quftan, two old friends of ours from Baghdad. The doctor came to be on very good terms with Fournier immediately, because his hobby too was playing the violin; so he became part of the landlord's string ensemble consisting of amateurs who met in his room a few nights per week. Another apartment would be taken by Basim Hannoush, who was studying for a doctorate in economics. In addition to these, there was an American student called Carol and next to her a German student called Hans, who was attracted to her. In the basement lived two young Canadian sisters, who were very helpful and whose greatest delight, especially Marianne, was that one of the tenants invite them for a cup of coffee.

The apartments were generally small and without kitchens. However, our apartment consisted of one large room, a bathroom, and a simply equipped kitchenette. When Lamiᶜa was faced with the necessity of preparing meals, it became clear that she did not know how to boil a couple of eggs, let alone to cook rice or make a broth, so she sought guidance from cookbooks . . .

In addition to three comfortable armchairs, we had a blue sofa on which we sat in the daytime. At night the sofa could be transformed into a bed, but it was an uncomfortable bed. So when it came time to sleep, we removed the cushions and bedding from the sofa and spread them on the floor, making them into a wide mattress with which we were happy in that charming paradise that we finally appropriated from a grim world crowded with human beings.

And no wonder, it was paradise; for soon afterwards, we were fortunate to have a number of the most wonderful friends in addition to those we had brought to live in the same house such as Tawfiq Sayigh, Munah Khouri, and Hasan Zakariyya (all of whom were unmarried) and two or three American doctoral students. As for me, I plunged headlong into my research with some of the most famous professors of literary criticism in contemporary literature; and my classmates were mostly teachers, novelists, and poets.

Not for a moment did we forget any of our dear ones and friends whom we had left in Baghdad. We noticed that, in the second half of 1952, all members of our group in Baghdad had experienced something like the happy endings found especially in Shakespeare's comedies, everyone's wishes and desires being suddenly fulfilled. After lovers had experienced love and its quarrels, mixups, threats of misery and wretchedness, fate would change direction and please this person and smile at the lovers, two by two, before turning to other people in other places.

Sahira was the first of our group to get married; her husband was a prominent professor at one of the colleges. Shortly afterwards, Dr. Isam married Anisa al-Sadoun a few days after she returned from her studies in America, and a big reception was held in their honor at the Alawiyya Club, which Lami^c^a and I attended with other friends. Then Lami^c^a and I got married, our marriage being rather like those in tales, and afterwards we went to Lebanon then to Harvard University, where I translated my first novel *Scream in a Long Night* into Arabic and where among critical studies and much fiction and poetry, I began to write in English my second novel *Hunters in a Narrow Street.*

As for Husayn Haddawi, after he and his wife and daughter accompanied us on our journey, he returned to the University of Nevada at Las Vegas to obtain a doctorate in the works of James Joyce and to become professor of English literature at that university.

Jawad Salim and his wife Lorna, who was in her final months of pregnancy, had their first child, a baby girl they named Zaynab. He carved a big statue of teak that he named *Motherhood,* which was one of his most beautiful and powerful works; he also made his statuette *The Political Prisoner,* which would make him, months later, one of the first winners of an international contest in London.

In addition to his work at the College of Medicine, Dr. Ali Kamal established himself in a private clinic overlooking King Faysal II Square, in what was at the time the heart of Baghdad. He soon became famous as one of the most prominent physicians in town and had a third daughter, Layla. He abstractedly and enthusiastically spoke of a series of books he would write one day, naming the series "Closed Doors of the Mind" (a project that he realized in a distinguished scientific manner thirty years later).

At Harvard we received good news in succession: Hilmi married Evelyn Dalali, Lamiᶜa's friend and professor of psychology at Queen Aliya College, and they went to live in Kirkuk where Hilmi had a position as a mathematician and engineer at the Iraq Petroleum Company and would soon be promoted and finally become general manager of the company. Widad, Evelyn's sister, married one of the professors of English literature at the Higher Teachers' College. As for Buland al-Haydari, he published his important poetry collection, *Aghani al-Madina al-Mayta* (Songs of the Dead City) with the introduction that I had written for it in 1949, and he married Dalal al-Mufti, the beautiful young woman we met with him at his sister Roxane's house in New Baghdad; she had graduated from the American University of Beirut and was full of admiration for his poetry; and they lived in a house opposite Adnan Raouf's and close to Lamiᶜa's home on Taha Street, to which we would return in March of 1954. Adnan Raouf married Sumayya al-Khaffaf, one of my outstanding students at Preparatory College in the years 1948 and 1949, and he went to work at the Ministry of the Exterior in Baghdad.

My faithful female student too was married in the same period to a handsome young man with a distinguished social position. My colleague Rosemary Boxer, the beautiful English woman who had come to us at Queen Aliya College from the University of Oxford to teach with me, she too got married; and her husband, Dr. Yousuf Sayigh, was the older brother of my friend Tawfiq Sayigh, a friend since our days together in Jerusalem. Dr. Sayigh's economic duties occasionally took him to Baghdad, where he met Rosemary, fell in love with her, and took her with him to live in Beirut.

While we were in America, Nizar Salim was transferred to a position outside Iraq in the context of his work at the Ministry of the Exterior, and he married a young German woman who encouraged him to begin painting in oil and water colors. Adnan, the lawyer, who was my rival for Lamiᶜa for some time and who imagined that his lack of English was the cause of his being disappointed, realized his heart's wish and traveled to America for further studies in law, then stayed permanently there after he married an American woman.

However, there remained one woman of our group who did not get married despite her education, prepossessing beauty, and graceful figure. She refused all those who asked for her hand because the only man she wished for as a husband had married a friend.

Qahtan Awni did not get married at this time, although we expected him to marry a beautiful young woman from Basra who stayed with us for several months. But he was too slow to act and one of her relatives grabbed her. Two or three years later, he finally married a beautiful woman, Malika Ibrahim Shawkat, soon after her return from her studies in America. Her father was from Baghdad and her mother was from Palestine.

We can claim that they all lived happily and realized many of their dreams in the years that followed.

■ ■ ■

Five or six weeks after all this bliss, we were shocked when Lami͑a received a telegram from her mother telling her of the necessity of her immediate return. She told her that the minister of education had published a notice in the Baghdad newspapers that said that Lami͑a must return immediately to her position by such-and-such a day. Otherwise, she would be considered to have resigned, and her guarantor (her mother) would have to pay back to the Iraqi treasury the amount of four thousand dinars, which was the amount spent by the government on Lami͑a's studies at the University of Wisconsin two or three years earlier. This meant that the minister had suddenly changed his mind concerning her accompanying me, which he had astonished us by approving in August and charmed us with his generosity. How could Lami͑a's mother or any other person pay that amount, an incredible sum in those days, when the salary of a professor with a master's degree was twenty-five dinars per month, and a professor's with a doctorate was thirty dinars?

We had to make plans and devise a way for Lami͑a to return by air somehow, but we did not have enough money for the travel expenses. However, the real difficulty as far as we were concerned was the separation that had suddenly been imposed on us as we were at the height of our happiness.

We knew that Nathir al-Umari had been transferred to Iraq's permanent delegation at the United Nations in New York. Since Lami^ca's trip back would begin in New York, I accompanied her to New York, and we stayed at Nathir and Mayy's home on Riverside Drive on the banks of the Hudson. We were very pleased to see them again in their home, and one evening, they took us to have dinner at the famous Rainbow Restaurant on the hundredth floor of the Empire State Building, which was then the world's tallest building. In the elevator with us was a tall, beautiful blond lady wearing an eye-catching fur coat. We immediately realized that it was the beloved actress Doris Day, and we exchanged greetings with her. Her appearance proudly and clearly declared: How wonderful it is for a woman to be both beautiful and famous!

The morning of the next day, Nathir took us to the office of the Iraqi delegation at the United Nations. We visited the UN buildings, distinguished by their architectural style and interior design, and we were introduced to several people. But our meeting with Ata Abd al-Wahhab, Nathir's colleague in the Iraqi delegation, was more important. His wife Batoul had been Lami^ca's friend since the days they were both students, and Lami^ca was related to Ata. We spent the evening as their guests, and Ata took us from one sumptuous restaurant to another with music and dancing until a late hour. And thus began an intimate friendship between Ata and me, like the one that existed between Nathir and me, that lasted over the years and still continues. As was his custom, Ata always combined an enthusiastic intellect and a considerable poetic talent with a brilliant sense of humor. With his amusing comments and continuous jokes, he was ever at the center of his circle of friends whenever they met for lunch or dinner.

■ ■ ■

Lami^ca reached Baghdad toward the end of the year, when the city was seething with political turmoil. Student strikes at the colleges and schools were so common that she could resume work only after several weeks. We had planned well: the amount of one hundred dollars that the Rockefeller Foundation paid her as a monthly allowance continued to be sent to her regularly. By June of 1953, she had saved enough money to buy an airline ticket so that we could spend the rest of the year together. I went again to New York and stayed with Nathir and Mayy; and the next morning, we all went to the airport together to greet Lamiᶜa, who was arriving from Paris. When she came down the steps in a wonderful dress that revealed her décolletage and arms, I could hardly believe my eyes: her figure looked like that of a Babylonian goddess. She was the most beautiful woman among all the women who came down those steps; she even was the most beautiful creature among all those we saw in the crowds at the airport. When I embraced her, I felt I was embracing the most desirable woman in the western hemisphere. And why would I not say in the eastern hemisphere too?

A day or two later, we hurried back to our apartment in Cambridge, Massachusetts, as though we were celebrating our honeymoon again, and our friends were waiting for us there. During the academic year's long evenings of study, we often prepared lunch for everyone consisting of chicken legs roasted in the oven in our kitchenette (we could buy ready-to-cook chicken legs from the nearby supermarket); or we made them Palestinian *mujaddara,* a dish made of rice, lentils, and onions cooked in water with olive oil, cumin, allspice, and salt, which I taught Lamiᶜa how to make according to how my mother cooked it.

One thing Lamiᶜa refused to learn: how to make coffee. I always made coffee for her and me, and I solemnly promised to continue making it as long as we lived. And so, I made our coffee every day . . . and I kept my promise for forty full years until the end.*

■ ■ ■

---

*Lamiᶜa predeceased Jabra. She died on October 14, 1992. In a letter to me from Baghdad dated February 7, 1993, Jabra wrote after seventeen months of no communication following the Gulf War, "I don't know whether you have learnt that my beloved wife died on 14 October last year leaving a terrible emptiness in my life, and that I had a heart attack days later and was taken to intensive care for a few days. . . ." See page 83 of my book in Arabic *al-Tajriba al-Jamila* (Beirut: al-Mu'assasa al-Arabiyya li-l-Dirasat wa-l-Nashr, 2001), containing Jabra's letters to me from 1966 to 1994. *(Translator's note.)*

When I returned to Baghdad at the beginning of spring in 1954, Lamiᶜa had preceded me and succeeded in her efforts to have the Iraq Petroleum Company keep the position vacant in its Public Relations Department that Frank Stokes wanted me to occupy. He continued to like what he read for me, especially after the narration I translated for Michael Clark's documentary on Iraqi oil, *The Third Tributary,* more than three and a half years earlier. It was strange how coincidence interwove in 1952 to result in my return to Baghdad, where I found waiting for me an enjoyable job at a good salary that gave Lamiᶜa the opportunity to leave her teaching later. I worked in a civilized atmosphere that helped me continue my intellectual activities as I wished, for about a quarter of a century.

One of the first people who visited me in my office after my appointment was Abd al-Hamid Rifat, Lamiᶜa's maternal uncle and the company's legal consultant. He congratulated me and laughed, saying, "Lamiᶜa married you against my advice and you were appointed to a post in this company without my advice . . . Isn't this what independence is all about?" A deep personal and family relationship immediately arose between us.

Upon my arrival, Lamiᶜa created for me the serene atmosphere full of color, movement, and beautiful people that we both liked; and I felt that, despite the difficulties and vexations that we had experienced and that no longer frightened us when they reoccurred, our life was beginning to be built on more love than we could ever imagine and on a confidence of a future in which friendships would continue and grow. We felt it was finally right for us to think of having children, trusting—although only for a time—that destiny would not betray us or them, even if we knew that we were somewhat deluding ourselves.

As far as I was concerned, writing and occasional painting were as necessary to me as love, friendship, and bread and water. Lamiᶜa knew all that and eagerly made sure I could do them. Without talking about it, and with a lot of sacrifice, she provided for me an atmosphere with spontaneity and taste. With her wide reading in Arabic and English, her very Iraqi and yet cosmopolitan views, and her critical eye that was not easily satisfied, she followed all that I wrote and all that I painted, and she always had her own enthusiastic and learned opinion.

She could be very angry at anything that did not please her and with anybody, man or woman, who did not satisfy her. But she never lost her ability to tolerate and forgive, and she always gave love the highest place in life, day after day, and year after year.

■ ■ ■

What I spoke about here is only the annus mirabilis 1951 and the year that followed and was similar to it: I wrote about just two years. I spoke sparingly, and because of all sorts of necessities, I neglected and deleted many things. Forty more years of marriage remain and demand that I speak of them. These two years were only a wonderful beginning, the starting point of a journey in time that we wanted to always remain on the cutting edge of the wonderful and the marvelous.

In a period that we wanted to fill with what was good and beautiful, evil was often mixed with good, and the ugly with the beautiful—despite our efforts to keep them at bay. It was one of the strangest periods of Arab history, which is replete with contradictions; it was also a period full of possibilities for joy and self-realization, alongside the dislocation, the terror, and the killing that it witnessed. Is there an end to speaking about all that? I have spoken about some aspects of it in my novels; I have sprinkled other aspects in my studies, essays, and interviews. But most will remain for someone who has the ability, the patience, the love to deduce it from letters, papers, and boundless other sources—if they are not dispersed by storms and drowned by floods, and remain intact for some researcher to refer to them, whether it be in the near or the far future.

February 27, 1994.